THE BOOK OF
ADDISCOMBE

The Book of
Addiscombe

Canning & Clyde Road Residents
Association & Friends

HALSGROVE

First published in Great Britain in 2000
Reprinted 2001.

THIS BOOK IS DEDICATED TO THE MEMORY OF THE LATE DORIS HOBBS AND VIC CHEAL. OUR THANKS TO THE MILLENNIUM AWARDS FOR ALL FOR ENCOURAGING THE PUBLICATION OF THIS BOOK. THEY REQUESTED THAT WE DID SOMETHING ENDURING FOR THE COMMUNITY AND WE HOPE THAT THIS IS A FITTING PROJECT.

British Library Cataloguing-in-Publication Data
A CIP record for this title is available from the British Library

ISBN 1 84114 094 5

Photograph previous page:
Folly Four 1929, Pagehurst Road. (J.G.)

HALSGROVE
PUBLISHING, MEDIA AND DISTRIBUTION

Halsgrove House
Lower Moor Way
Tiverton, Devon EX16 6SS
Tel: 01884 243242
Fax: 01884 243325
email: sales@halsgrove.com
website: http://www.halsgrove.com

Printed and bound in Great Britain by Bookcraft Ltd, Midsomer Norton.

FOREWORD

It is with pleasure that I write this foreword to *The Book of Addiscombe*. I recall being led by Doris Hobbs on several interesting walks along the history-packed streets as she unravelled its wonderful story. I have watched as big houses have become blocks of modern flats and have seen, with regret, the modernisation of the area.

There was much ground to cover – the churches, each a beautiful historic building in its own right, the transport, from horse-drawn vehicles through to the railways, trams and buses, and now, full circle, to trams again. There were also the communication systems from semaphore and morse to Creed's telegraph systems. The East India Company both at home and in far-away Eastern countries must have used some of these. Their college for training the cadets had a great impact on the area. People from all walks of life through times of war and peace have told their stories.

The challenge to record the past history of Addiscombe has been grasped ably by Steve Collins, Anne Bridge and the Canning & Clyde Road Residents Association, greatly helped by John Gent and many other contributors. The resultant book is a joy to read and to have on your coffee table to dip into at leisure. There is enough history here to make a film! I congratulate all concerned and thank them for taking time to produce this book. Well done all of you.

MAY JOHNSON,
CHAIRMAN, THE CROYDON SOCIETY

John Horrocks Joinery Works, Oval Road, 1908. (J.G.)

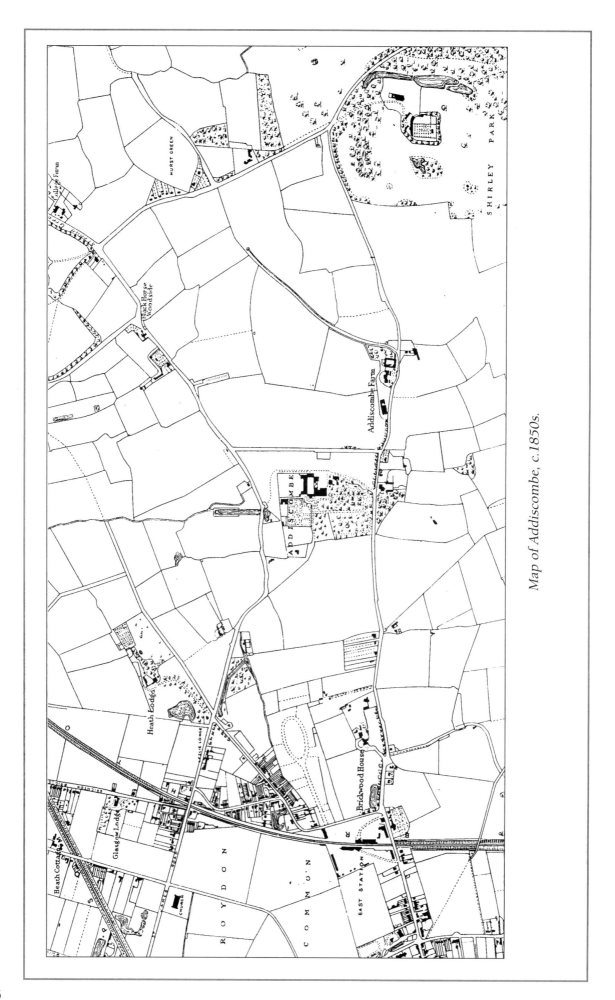

Map of Addiscombe, c.1850s.

CONTENTS

 **Anne Bridge** was born in Orpington and to her amazement ended up in Croydon. She has lived in Canning Road for the last six years. Anne was fascinated by the eccentric architecture of St Mary Magdalene and this is how she first started to discover the local history of Addiscombe. She was a teacher for eight years and now works for a charity. Her main interests are photography and music.

Deborah Bryan was born and raised in Clapham but has lived in Addiscombe for 11 years. She is a barrister practising in the Temple and specialises in the field of  family law. Deborah is also a jazz fan whose interests include modern art and design, eating out, travel and cookery.

Victor (Vic) Raymond Cheal was born on 25 June 1940 and spent his early years in Cranbrook, Kent, where he followed his father as a Telecoms Engineer. As a young man he was also active in amateur dramatics, rugby football and his masonic lodge. In 1966 he joined the Post Office Investigation Department (POID) in which he served for 30 years. Vic also gained a commission as a Captain in the Territorial Army (REPS) during that time. In the POID Vic served all over the UK and was promoted to Senior Investigation Officer. He was always noted for his devotion to duty and for the courtesy and consideration he showed to others.

Unfortunately Vic developed Multiple Sclerosis in the 1990s and had to retire on health grounds in 1996. In retirement he remained active in his old comrades association and in local community affairs, including writing a contribution to this book which he completed on the very day of his fatal collapse. Vic died on 25 May 2000. He was a most gregarious, kind and generous man. Despite having no surviving family members, Vic's funeral was a memorable celebration of his life, attended by some 170 friends and former colleagues.

 **Steve Collins** formed the Canning & Clyde Road Residents Association in 1979. He has lived in Croydon for over 30 years and in Canning Road for the last 23. He has long taken an active and practical interest in the community. Steve operates a computer business from Canning Road and is an inveterate inventor. His interests include music, especially blues, rock and jazz. His annual live music parties have become a local legend. Ask anyone!

David Delaney initially lived in Croydon between 1943 and 1961. Having moved away for while, he returned for a further seven years. David has lived on a canal boat and now spends his time between Croydon and the canals. He has a lot of practical experience of canals and canal boats and is interested in canal restoration. David has also done a lot of canal towpath walking. He was fascinated to discover that Croydon had once had a canal and despite having lived here for so long, he did not know about this until he had his own boat. David has produced a concise, remarkable, information packed video outlining the canal route and its history.

 **Steve Earl** is the Chairman and founder member of the South Eastern and Chatham Railway Preservation Society Limited which hopes to purchase Addiscombe Station and its EMU shed for housing their collection of railway artefacts from the early 1800s to the present day. Steve has a keen interest in history and he is one of the curatorial staff of the Metropolitan Police Historical Museum.

Isha Shona Gabrielle was born on 5 September 1985 in Preston, Lancashire and moved to Feltham in Middlesex in 1987. In primary school she revealed a great talent for sport before going on to the Green School for Girls in Isleworth.

Isha moved to Croydon in June 1998 and began at Ashburton Community School in September 1999. A school librarian and member of the School Council and a Peer Mentor she recently took part in project training and peer mentoring at school. Isha is studying Business Studies and Geography as well as the compulsory GCSE subjects. She loves reading books and magazines, music, singing and swimming.

John Gent is a wonderfully nice man – gent by name, gent by nature. His help with this book has been invaluable. He was born in 1932 in South Norwood and has lived in the Croydon area ever since. He attended Cyprus Road and Selhurst Grammar Schools and, following National Service in the Royal Air Force, joined London Transport in 1952. In 1990 he decided to retire to devote more time to local history research and his other interests.

It was in the late 1940s that John became fascinated by local history and he has written and edited many illustrated books, including for the Croydon Natural History and Scientific Society which he joined in 1959. He has twice been president of that society and was founder chairman of the Croydon Society. John has lectured extensively on various aspects of Croydon's history and has been a member of the Surrey Local History Council since 1975. He has collected postcards and old photographs for over 50 years and among his other interests he includes photography, walking, music, gardening, transport and model railways.

Quite simply, this book would not have been possible without John's assistance. Thank you.

Doris Courtney Helmke Hobbs was born in 1917 near Sittingbourne, Kent, but lived in Croydon virtually all her life. She attended Beulah School, Thornton Heath, from 1923 until she left aged 14 at Easter 1931. Doris worked for a while at Creed's teleprinter factory in Cherry Orchard Road and remained in touch with Mrs Creed, a neighbour, for many years. Doris lived in Addiscombe from 1942. From about 1956 she began recording the changing

face of Croydon in photographs. Ten years later she became a traffic warden which afforded excellent opportunities to continue in this project. With her interest in local history Doris joined the Croydon Society in 1967 where she was very active. Her research into the history of the roads around where she lived proved fruitful and she is remembered vividly by those who followed her historical 'town trails' around Addiscombe and Woodside.

Between 1968 and 1971 Doris was a Conservative Councillor and during this time she campaigned for a local museum of Croydon. In 1973 she was promoted to the post of Traffic Warden Controller at London's largest traffic warden centre at Oxford Circus.

In retirement Doris took a Diploma in English Local History. Her dissertation into 19th-century Addiscombe centred on the East India Company land and forms the backbone of chapter 4.

Doris died suddenly on 6 October 1987 aged 70. Those who met her remember her well. Her obituary in *Croydon and Croydonians*, the journal of the Croydon Natural History and Scientific Society Ltd., from which most of the above notes are taken, ends 'Doris Hobbs was, within the Society and within Croydon at large, a challenging and thought-provoking personality. She had a deep-rooted ability to bring history to life for ordinary people. She will be missed by many'.

After working in the insurance industry, **John Hobbs** has retired. For a number of years he has been collecting historic postcards and pictures of the Croydon area. He shares this interest in local history with his wife, Christine. John and his son, Steven, witnessed the demolition of the historic Bingham Road Bridge.

Paul Nihill was Addiscombe's and Croydon's first ever Olympic medallist. In 1964 he won a silver medal in Tokyo for the 50km walk. During a  distinguished athletic career he has held world records for the 3km and 5km track and the 20km and 30km road walks. Now living in the Medway area, Paul still plays an active role in local sports clubs. In 1976 he was awarded the MBE for services to sport.

Paul is enthusiastically interested in the history of Addiscombe of which he has fond memories. Now living in Rochester, he retains an active interest in local sport and returns to Croydon at least once a month.

Stephen Parascandolo was born on 20 October 1980 in Lewisham, South East London and now lives in West Wickham, Kent. He is currently studying for a BEng in Computer Systems Engineering at Brunel University, Uxbridge and hopes to work in the computer industry

A keen transport enthusiast, he became particularly interested in modern light rail with the advent of the construction of the Croydon Tramlink system fairly close to home. In February 1999 he set up an unofficial website for the system at http://www.croydon-tramlink.co.uk and has been amazed by the response, which in the week before opening was achieving 400 visitors a day!

David Payne has lived in Addiscombe all of his life and has many stories to tell. He is keenly interested in the history of the borough. See the section on Leslie Park Road where we feature his business and memories of life in Addiscombe.

Tony Stelling was born in 1935 at St Mary's in Croydon and lived in Upper Norwood. During the war years his family lived in a Hampshire village. Returning to Croydon in 1945 he attended Selhurst Grammar School for boys until 1953, when he joined the Royal Signals for his National Service. In 1955 he started his career in industry as a Student Apprentice at GEC Coventry, and spent most of his working life with Mullard and Philips in Stockport. In 1985 he returned to Croydon, to work at Mullard's HQ in London. In 1989 he joined Landis & Gyr at Purley Way (previously AGI). He retired last year, and lives with his wife Barbara in 'Upper Addiscombe'. Their two children have both flown the nest, and are now married.

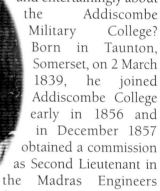

So who was **Colonel Vibart** who wrote so expansively and entertainingly about the Addiscombe Military College? Born in Taunton, Somerset, on 2 March 1839, he joined Addiscombe College early in 1856 and in December 1857 obtained a commission as Second Lieutenant in the Madras Engineers under the East India Company. Although in the Army, he was never on active military duties but spent his career on civil duties as an engineer, principally concerned with constructing irrigation works. During his entire adult life he travelled extensively in India and on the Continent. On 24 December 1884 Vibart married Miss Le Hardy, whose father was in the Madras Engineers. The couple had two daughters, who died in infancy, and a son who later joined the British Expeditionary forces. Vibart retired on 12 December 1891, having already settled in Cornwall Gardens, London SW1, early that year. In 1905 Vibart and his wife left Cornwall Gardens to travel widely on the continent before settling in Henley-on-Thames. In 1916 Vibart suffered a severe attack of influenza from which he never fully recovered and he died on 1 November 1917.

Vibart has been described as being of a strong, straightforward character. He hated injustice and was fiercely loyal to his friends. Vibart could be combative and would not hesitate to launch an attack on the authorities in defence of friends, colleagues or himself, if he felt they had not been fairly treated. He spoke his mind very plainly, which did not always go down well with his superiors and probably had an adverse effect on his career. For all this, Vibart was hospitable and had a great sense of humour.

Peter Walker was born at a tram terminus in Birmingham in 1933, trained as an architect but preferred transport engineering, town planning, journalism, music, history and an occasional drink. He moved to Croydon in the 1960s and since retirement has devoted himself to local history.

OTHER CONTRIBUTORS INCLUDE:

Linda Bailey, Simone Bailey & Doug, Basil Baker, Alma Boxhall, British Library, Barbara Broughton, Charles Budden, Dudley Cary, Nigel J. Clarke, Bob Corner, *Croydon Advertiser*, Croydon Airport Society, Croydon Local Studies Library, Barry Hall, Edward Handley, Diane Hills, Steven Hobbs, George Hoole, Barbara Howard, Rosa Hurn, May Johnson, Peter Little, Cyril Lloyd, Kay Manley, Geoffrey Moir, Jonathan Moore, Paul O'Callaghan, Richard Ogden, Mr Pentecost, Susan Pope, Brian Richardson, St Mildred's Parish Council, Royal Society of Arts, Roy Sealey, Sandy Skinner, Peter Smith, Ruth Sowan, Edna and Ted Thomas, Ruth Watts, Peter Whybrow, Tony Wild, Peter Stanley Williams, Bill Wood, Elna Wood, Daniel and David Wright, Revd J. Wright.

Sincere apologies for any omissions. Thank you everyone for all of your help.

Ashburton House. (J.G.) *The Ashburton Estate lay on the area now bounded by Addiscombe Road, Lower Addiscombe Road, Shirley Road and Ashburton Road. The actual house was at the junction of Addiscombe Road and what is now Northampton Road. It was built in the late 1700s by John Dunning, Whig politician and lawyer who married Elizabeth Baring of the banking family. When Alexander Baring became a peer in 1838, he took over the vacant barony of Ashburton in Devon, hence the name of the estate. He married Anne Louise Bingham and was succeeded by his son, William. Lady Ashburton died in 1857 and William remarried. When he died in 1864 the house went to his second wife who took an interest in child welfare and in 1880 started a Holiday Home for the Poor. She died in 1903; the house was pulled down in 1911/12 and the estate sold for housing.* (Information C.L.S.L.)

Two maps of 1868. (C.L.S.L.)

Introduction

Welcome to *The Book of Addiscombe*, a wander through the questions of when, what, why and how. Here we have concentrated on Addiscombe but on occasion, we touch on adjacent areas and events that have made Addiscombe what it is today. We have discovered that some residents in Woodside and Shirley consider themselves to be 'Addiscombians'.

Essentially the boundaries of the book lead from the Addiscombe Road, through part of Park Hill and Shirley, Ashburton and Woodside, out to the Croydon Canal and Morland Road before running back to Lower Addiscombe Road, East Croydon Station and the Addiscombe Road again - a considerable area to cover.

We apologise where any person, place, event or piece of history has been omitted - we have, however, done our best to be as comprehensive and accurate as possible. Where doubt arises as to certain facts, we will confess and leave you with the clues to find out more for yourselves. Please let us know how you get on! It is hard to believe the number of remarkable people and events that we have discovered in our research for this volume. The project was spurred on by many people's enquiries about the history of the area and we thought that it was about time such a study was written.

We are indebted to a great many people and organisations for all of their assistance. Of particular note are the late, great Doris Hobbs, Col Henry M. Vibart and the truly superb Croydon Local Studies Library which, we understand, is reckoned to be the second best in the U.K. We think that it is probably the best!

And a very special word for John Gent who, as his name implies, is indeed a perfect gentleman and a superb local historian and picture archivist.

Detail from a Luftwaffe aerial reconnaissance photograph taken on 8 September 1940.

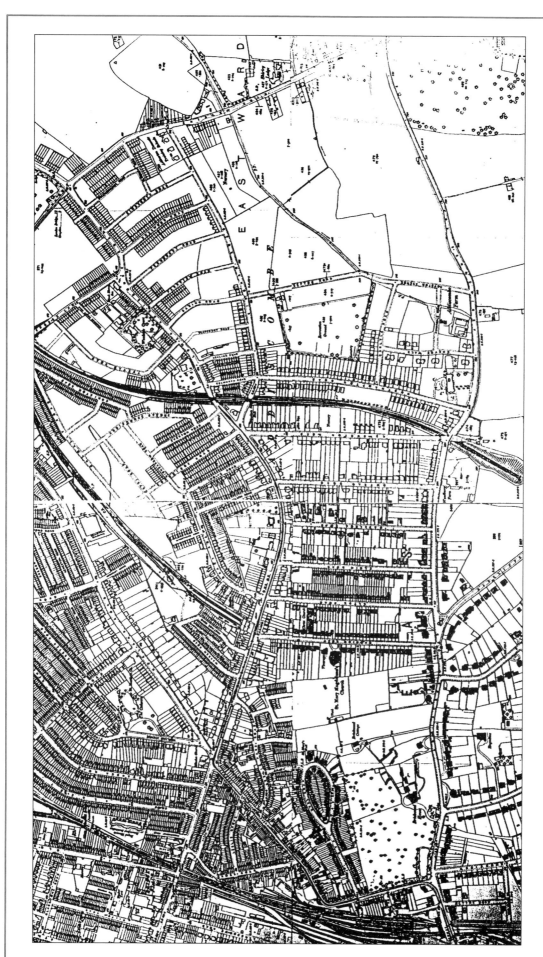

Map of 1913. (C.L.S.L.)

His generous encouragement and help with both pictures and words have been invaluable. Thanks also to the some 50 or so local inhabitants as well as those from further afield who have made contributions to this book (see page 9 for details). Thanks to Tony Stelling for his superb research of sometimes confusing official Second World War records that he has cross referenced with local people in order to establish what really happened. Nor should we forget Tony's heroic grappling with 'lineart' scans on our behalf. We thank the Millennium Awards for All Commission for providing us with the funds so

that we might more ably compile, publish and distribute this book.

So where do we start? We have Canning Road, Clyde Road, Elgin Road, Havelock Road, Outram Road, Warren Road, Hastings Road and many more – names associated with India, which is, in essence, where our story will start. We will tell you how the area grew up from farmland through East India Company times, how it fared through the First and Second World Wars and why it looks as it does today.

This book is dedicated in particular to the memory of Doris Hobbs and Vic Cheal.

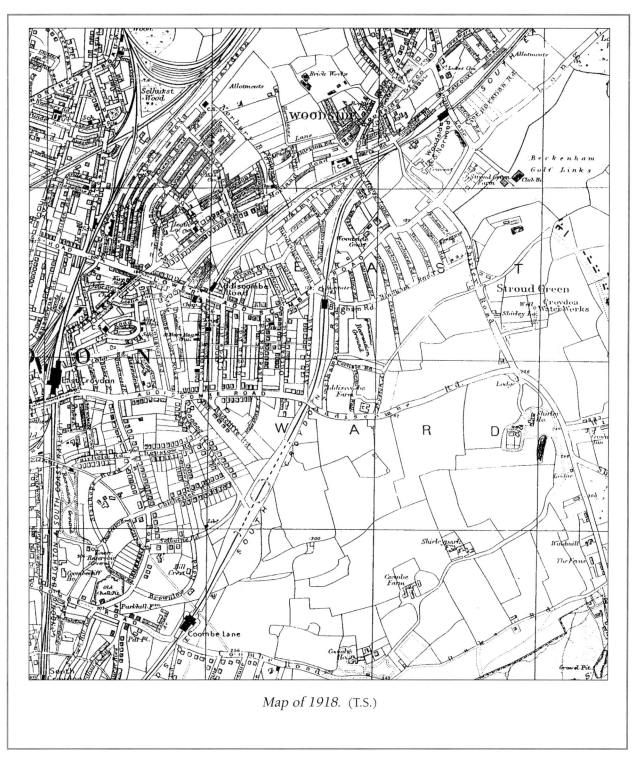

Map of 1918. (T.S.)

Top: *Addiscombe Farm, 1907.* (J.H.)

Opposite page: *Addiscombe Farm, 1896.* (J.G.)

Above: *Map showing Addiscombe Farm, 1896.*

Right: *Another map showing Addiscombe Farm, 1912.* (Both C.L.S.L.)

Chapter 1
Addiscombe Farm

by Deborah Bryan

The Ashburton family owned a fairly grand home which included a farmhouse on the same land. The Addiscombe farmhouse was built in 1676. The original flint work remains at the front of the house and the date has been clearly inscribed in red bricks between the upstairs front windows.

The original building consisted of a two-storey structure with a central entrance and an end chimney. There were two rooms on each storey. Service rooms were added later to the area which now contains the staircase and one original bread oven with a heavy 'carron' iron door. A further addition to the east of the house was a dairy which had a stone flagged floor. The interior walls are partially covered with the most attractive hand-painted tiles, 57 of which are illustrated with decorative birds, each painted differently. There are also plain tiles together with geometrically decorated ones which are thought to be Portuguese in origin. There is evidence that this area of the house was used as a shop where locals would purchase bread and dairy products. On the ground floor the room situated to the west contains an inglenook fireplace which was uncovered in 1950 by the then owners of the property. It is apparent that the brick area originally contained an oven.

The farmhouse is a Grade II listed building with deeds that date back to 1676, although previous owners have thought it to be older in parts. It was part of the farm leased by William Marshall who wrote 'Minutes of Agriculture... near Croydon Surrey'. The outbuildings included cowsheds which spread east as far as what is now Fryston Avenue. Marshall used the farm buildings but lived at Home Farm which has since been destroyed.

J.J. Parson's cow, Mayflower, prize-winner at the Croydon Horse Show, 1908. (J.G.)

Carting hay, Park Hill, c.1910. (J.G.)

Chapter 2
From the Year Dot

by Kay Manley and Anne Bridge

WHAT'S IN A NAME?

Addiscombe is situated one mile east of Croydon town centre and was in ancient times one of the seven boroughs of Croydon. There are various theories surrounding the origin of the name. 'Addiscombe' comes from Old English and is composed in the first part of 'Aeddi', a personal name, and secondly 'camp', meaning an enclosed piece of land. Therefore it is the place where Aeddi lived. The nearby village of Addington may have been settled by the same family. Another explanation surrounds the word 'combe' - the Anglo-Saxon version of the Welsh word 'cumb' meaning a 'hollow in a hill'. Addiscombe is a place on the edge of the valley between Croham Hurst and Norwood. Other spellings of Addiscombe have been: Edgcumb, Edgecombe, Adgcomb, Adscumb, Adscombe, Addscomb and Addescombe, and today's spelling evolved from Edescamp in 1229 to the recognisable form by 1721.

OF KINGS, PLOTS AND PARLIAMENTS

The Herons   The first established dwelling of any size appears to have been erected by Thomas Heron during the reign of Henry VII and was known as Adgcomb. The foundations, walls and relics of this building were discovered in comparatively recent times. Thomas fell under the displeasure of the king (it is said for his support of Perkin Warbeck, who claimed he was the Duke of York and therefore had more right to the throne of England) and the lands were conceded to a Humphrey Wilde.

However, by the time that Henry VIII was on the throne, it all seems to have blown over for we find that Thomas Heron (son) was by this time in possession after the death of his father in 1516. Thomas rebuilt the mansion, now called 'Addescombe', on a much grander scale. According to records of the time, he was a man of high standing in the county of Surrey, and Thomas Cromwell, then agent for Cardinal Wolsey, stayed with him for some reason. Thomas Heron was laid to rest at Croydon Parish Church, a privilege granted to his family because they owned the Parsonage or Rectory.

His eldest son, William, then succeeded to the property but, although he was happily married to Alice, they had no children, making his brother Nicholas the heir. Nicholas and his wife, Mary, had five sons and eight daughters. Nicholas received a knighthood before his death in 1568 and, when Dame Mary passed on, Captain Poynings Heron came into the property.

Captain Poynings Heron was a professional soldier, serving for many years in the Low Countries for Elizabeth I. He did not therefore live at Addescombe Place but leased it to the Sonds family from Throwley in Kent. Poynings came home to die some years later and willed his estate to his eldest son, William, but the Sonds family continued to live there until 1594 when poor Lady Sonds went out of her mind. Her father and two brothers took over her affairs and they made a mark in history themselves, being imprisoned with Sir Walter Raleigh and George Brookes in connection with a plot over the succession of James I to the English throne. Brookes was beheaded but the Cobhams and Raleigh were given eleventh-hour reprieves. James I seized Addescombe Place and granted it to Sir Edward and Walter Barrett for the remainder of the Cobham lease.

Tunstall, Temple and Draper   When the lease expired in 1624, the house and lands were sold to Sir John Tonstall, or Tunstall, gentleman user to Queen Anne, James I's consort. The Tunstall family were connected with Addescombe Place for many years. They were staunchly royalist and after the Civil War became greatly impoverished, with the result that they had to sell Addescombe Place to Sir Purbeck Temple. This gentleman was a member of the Privy Council in the time of Charles II and held Addescombe Place for many years. He also owned land adjoining belonging to the Whitgift Hospital, from which an attempt was made to evict him 'for cutting down too many trees, and grubbing up the woodland'.

It seems that Sir Purbeck and Dame Sarah had no children and their heir was her nephew, William Draper. William was married to Susannah, daughter of the celebrated writer and diarist, Sir John Evelyn, founder of the Royal Society and friend of Samuel Pepys. Sir John noted that 'Sir Purbeck Temple had a great funeral at Addescombe.' He added, 'There being no heir, my son (in-law) Draper hopes for good fortune.' The estate did indeed pass to William Draper in 1700 and he demolished the old building and in 1702 had a large Palladian style mansion built after a design by Sir John Vanbrugh, architect of Blenheim Palace and Castle Howard. This mansion stood on the area that is now Havelock and Outram Roads. The mansion was lavish, the external walls cased with Portland stone and internal walls, ceilings and grand fireplace decorated by Sir James Thornhill who was responsible for the banqueting hall at Greenwich. John Evelyn described the new Addiscombe Place as 'one of the very best gentleman's houses in Surrey'.

LORDS, A PRIME MINISTER AND REVELRY

When William Draper died in 1718, he left the estate to his son of the same name. William Draper (son) did not live there but leased it to various notables, including Lord Chancellor Talbot who died in 1737.

This William Draper had no children and passed on the estate to his nephew, Charles Clark, who lived there until 1778. Charles Clark's wife continued to live there but, after her death, it passed to their grandson, Charles James Clark. This gentleman did not live there but leased Addiscombe Place to Charles Jenkinson, later Lord Liverpool. He was a member of

William Pitt, the Younger's, ministry, and rumours abounded of rousing parties there. A poem was written in celebration of the incident when William Pitt, while Prime Minister, rode back to London in such an inebriated state that he forgot to stop at a toll and was fired on by the watchman.

Charles James Clark died in an accident in Paris and the Addiscombe Estate passed to his sister, by then married to a member of the Radcliffe family, keeper of the King's Stud (George IV). When Charles Jenkinson died in 1808, the then owner, Henry Emilius Delme-Radcliffe, sold the estate to the East India Company for £15 500 plus £1104.10s.0d. for the timber and standing trees.

From 1808 until the present day our story becomes one of innovation and enterprise, of communication and community. The Addiscombe Estate was bought by the East India Company in 1808 and finally sold to developers in 1861. Today what was the Addiscombe Estate is that block of land running west to east and encompassing the Canning, Clyde, Elgin, Havelock, Outram and Ashburton Roads. It is bounded to the north by the Lower Addiscombe Road, including a triangular plot extending from Canning to Leslie Park Road, and to the south by Addiscombe Road. As, however, the area was developed in Victorian times, so we widen our focus to the places, people and supplies that made it all possible. In some respects it was the new town development of the time – everything happened quickly and this is where the story begins. We hope that you enjoy it!

Addiscombe Place, built in 1702.

Chapter 3
East India Company

by Col H.M. Vibart, Anne Bridge and Steve Collins
with thanks to Tony Wild and Doris Hobbs

Established as a trading company by Royal Charter in 1600 during the reign of Queen Elizabeth I, the company was variously known as 'The Governor and Company of Merchants of London trading into the East Indies', 'The United Company of Merchants of England trading to the East Indies', 'The East India Company', 'The Honourable East India Company' and 'John Company' (possibly derived from 'jehan', or 'powerful' as in Shah Jehan or Jehangir), or simply 'The Company'.

It has been described as the largest multinational business that the world has even seen. And indeed at its peak, in comparative terms, it would currently have dwarfed the combined might and activities of Microsoft, Coca Cola, and a few oil companies put together. 'The Company' was seriously big!

The East India Company played a formative role in the development of the world as we know it today. It gradually controlled over half the world's trade and a quarter of its population. In its heyday the company ran its own army and navy, minted its own currency and traded in every corner of the globe.

Its trading and influence were particularly strong in the East - China, Malaysia, Singapore, Burma and especially India including what is today Pakistan - and extended as far as the United States.

Little did the founders suspect that over the course of time the company would, amongst other historical events, be directly responsible for the Chinese Opium Wars, precipitating the Boston Tea Party and get saddled with minding Napoleon during his exile on St Helena! And there's much more.

The company was for two centuries primarily concerned with trading, but the imperial notions

The Hairy Family of Mandalay (Burma) - discovered by the company on their travels. Two Burmese wars (1824 and 1852-53) enabled the Company's annexation of Assam (a potentially profitable tea trade) and secured the coast of the Indian Ocean from Singapore to the north of the Indus.

and machinations of Clive (Baron Clive of Plassey 1725-74, depending on your view either General and statesman or ambitious and greedy individual), coupled with a collapse of predicted revenues in 1770 led to a disastrous fall in the value of stock, resulting in the company's request for a government loan of £1 million and Lord North's Regulating Act in 1773. This marked the beginning of government influence and was a contributing factor to the change in the nature of the company. Parliament terminated the company's monopoly on the Indian trade in 1813 and in its opening up to competition, recognised that the company's interests in India were now principally those of a ruler with which trading was considered incompatible - its nature had thus been transformed. The company ruled India until 1858 when, following the Indian Mutiny, the India Bill was passed and all the company's assets were vested in the Queen.

This transition to an agent of government was well under way during the period of Addiscombe College, 1809 to 1858. The Indian Army held many attractions for European officers. Unlike the Crown Army, commissions were not bought but achieved on merit - an opportunity which was seized upon by the ambitious sons of the middle class. Indeed, at Addiscombe, the standards of entrance were high and the cadets underwent half-yearly public exams with no second chances. Since commissions could not be sold, officers would try to make as much money as possible while on active service; the batta (field allowances) were generous and exploited to the full, and backhanders on supply and transport were the norm. Prize money and other bounty further supplemented the regular pay.

Tiger hunting from the safety of the back of an elephant from Oriental Field Sports. (T.W.C.I.H.C.)

The Prince's first tiger with Edward future Emperor top left. (T.W.C.I.H.C.)

If you'd like to learn more of the exploits of the East India Company abroad, then Tony Wild's informative and entertaining book *The East India Company, Trade and Conquest from 1600* will leave you fully informed.

Previously the East India cadets had been trained by arrangement between the Crown Army and the East India Company at the Royal Military Academy at Woolwich. As the company's governing role increased, this was no longer considered sufficient, so the Addiscombe Place estate came on to the market at an opportune time when the company was considering setting up its own academy. The original land which they bought stretches approximately between what is now Canning Road and Ashburton Road but it was later expanded. The estate was purchased in December 1808 and the first entry of cadets were in residence by January 1809, although the business arrangements with Henry Emilius Delme-Radcliffe (note the name) were not completed until January 1810, the military college having been in residence for a year before the estate was formally handed over.

In the beginning everyone was crowded into the mansion but work soon started on the erection of barrack blocks, classrooms, hospital, laundry, bakehouse, brewhouse and other necessary buildings. All of these were eventually completed by 1828 at a cost of £21 397 by one Mr George Harrison. Greenhouses, fruit trees and asparagus beds were also established. Part of the grounds contained the parade ground and flagstaff, gun battery and bastion.

In order to become as self sufficient as possible, farmland to the north of the estate was initially rented from Mr Delme-Radcliffe in 1826 and used for growing food. It was eventually purchased in 1850. This farmland stretched roughly from what is now Warren Road to Inglis Road. About two-thirds of the total land was used as a farm while the remainder, some 30 acres, formed the grounds of the college with the mansion house in the middle. As far as it was possible, the college would appear to be self-contained, providing for itself. Although by the middle of the 19th century Croydon was well served by local tradesmen, builders, carpenters, tin- and range-smiths and so forth, there is no proof of any local retailers dealing with the College Steward. It is possible that the East India Company, being London based, would have had their own contractors providing for their several establishments. The college authorities did, however, allow certain local individuals, small tradesman, to enter their premises to sell minor items to the cadets who were allowed only a maximum half-a-crown ($12\frac{1}{2}$ pence) per week. More of these local individuals later.

The estate being on a south to north downward slope, there was no surface water nor any wells, although from time immemorial owners had been permitted to lay pipes and draw water from the large pond to the north of the estate called the Coldstream, in Canal Mead (sometimes called the Conduit Field).

This is where the Academy Gardens estate now stands. The engineer cadets used the water for bathing, practising bridge building and pontooning

Unloading tea-ships in the East India docks, 1867. (T.I.L.N.)

and – at the time – all of the Chief Engineers in the provinces of India were ex-Addiscombe men.

The last building of note to be erected was the large gym in 1851 which still stands today in Havelock Road. Erected near the Lower Lodge it included a fine large room with boarded floor, which contained apparatus for gymnastics and was supplied with foils and so forth for fencing, single sticks, etc.

The other remaining buildings that still exist from the East India Company days are the two semi-detached professors' houses, called Ashleigh 1 and 2,

which stand on the corner of Clyde Road and Addiscombe Road.

In 1837 the Court of Directors were worried to learn that the South Eastern Railway Company projected an amendment to their line so as to pass through Addiscombe. The college opposed the project as the property would be materially injured, it would involve discontinuing mortar practice and the comfort of the whole establishment would be much affected. It was not until two years later that the South Eastern Railway Company abandoned its project.

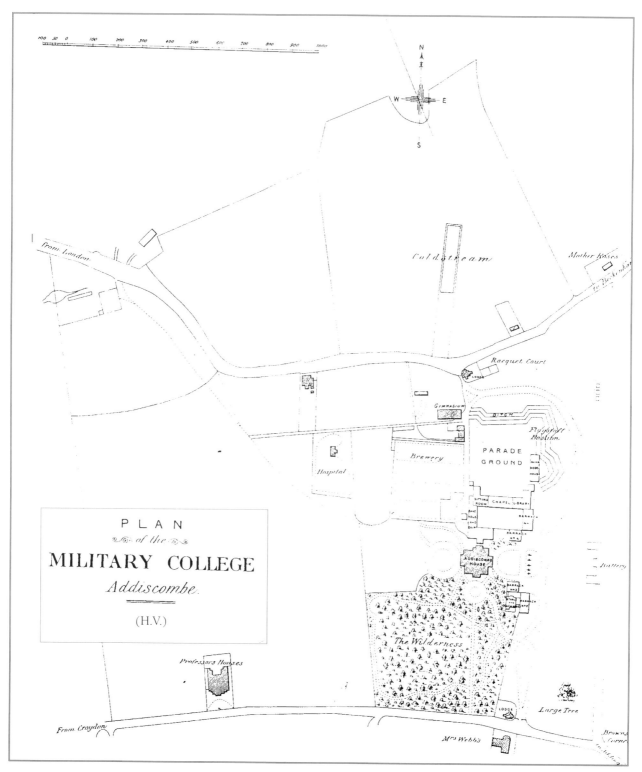

LIFE AT ADDISCOMBE COLLEGE

The instruction given to the cadets was of a scientific nature suitable for future engineers, surveyors and artillerymen, but seven years after the college's inception infantrymen were accepted. The course lasted for two years, each of four terms. Cadets were aged between 14 and 18. Entry was by way of public examination with further public examinations at the end of each term. Failure meant immediate expulsion from the college! The college was run on full military lines from the Lieut-Governor, always a soldier, to the sergeants who kept discipline and the cadets who obeyed orders. They were 'enjoined to conduct themselves respectfully' and were 'further cautioned against quarrelling, fighting and loose or improper language to one another.'

The professors in the classrooms were of the highest quality obtainable, the mathematics masters were all wranglers (ie with 1st class Honours Maths from Cambridge) and some professors were recognised in outside civilian life. An example was John Christian Schetky, a Hungarian born in Edinburgh, who joined the staff in 1837 as drawing master. In 1815 he had been appointed Painter in Watercolours to the Duke of Clarence, later William IV, and in 1830 Marine Painter to George IV.

Professor John Frederick Daniell, Lecturer in Chemistry, was a Fellow of the Royal Society and Professor at King's College. In 1845 David Thomas Ansted was appointed Lecturer on Geology; he was a geologist of considerable reputation, Fellow of the Royal Society and Professor at King's College, London. More significant was William Sturgeon, Lecturer in Science and Philosophy, who during his time at Addiscombe made significant advances in the field of electricity and magnetism. More of him later.

As future engineers and surveyors the cadets were well drilled in drawing (design before building) to the highest engineering standards. Practical work included bridge building and pontooning and fortification in the Sand Modelling Hall.

Other subjects included classics, French and Hindustani. Hindustani apparently was not a popular subject. Some cadets dreading the public examination in this subject used to contract 'Hindustani Fever' in order to be hospitalised and escape the exam. Just before seeing the doctor they would put chalk on their tongues or knock their elbows sharply against a wall so that their pulse became more rapid.

A day at the college was a regimented affair beginning at 6.00a.m. The cadets had lessons and parades and slept in dormitories, each having a 'kennel' 9 feet by 6 feet. Typical meals were: breakfast: tea and bread and butter, or bread and milk, if preferred; lunch: bread and cheese with good table beer; dinner: beef, mutton and veal alternately of the best kind, with the occasional change to pork when in season; tea: bread and butter, or bread and cheese with beer, if preferred.

At any one time there were about 150 cadets in residence at the college and during the 52 years of its existence about 3600 attended and were commissioned for service in India.

Above: Sand Modelling Hall and Barracks 1,2 and 4. Around 1839 Lt Cook, RN, FRS, Assistant Professor of Fortification, introduced the method of instruction in fortification by the use of models of works constructed of sand. In 1843 a Sand Modelling Hall was constructed, 60' by 50', roofed with corrugated iron and supported on light iron trusses (advanced for its time).
Top: John Christian Schetky, drawing master appointed in 1837.
Teachers were of the highest quality. (Both H.V.)

☙ Addiscombe ❧ College

Left: *The gymnasium still stands in Havelock Road, July 2000.* (S.C.)

Below: *Arcade in Study Court.* (H.V.)

Above: *Lower Lodge (on Lower Addiscombe Road between what are now Havelock and Outram Roads).*

Right: *Upper Lodge and Mrs Webb's (on Addiscombe Road near what is now Outram Road).*

Below: *'The Rosh'. Cadets play a friendly game of football with referee in full uniform.* (All H.V.)

GOOD TIMES - FUN STUFF

All of this hard work does not mean that the cadets did not have fun. The boys also enjoyed various games, football being the most popular. The Addiscombe College version of football (called 'The Rosh') was in fact a free-for-all:

You might kick the ball or hit it, catch it or pick it up and run with it. You might assault an adversary in any way and in any part of the field no matter how far you were from the ball, you might hack him or knock him down, you might handle him with one arm or two, seize him by the throat, throw him in the air, stamp on him when he was down, rub his nose in the ground.

Cricket was not nearly as popular, although athletics were. The cadets practised a little boxing. Billiards and pool were favourite games in the 1840s and '50s with cadets making for the King's Arms in Croydon for this. In order to secure a table there, the cadets would despatch their fastest runner after Parade. On occasions this would also entail some dodging of officers and teachers in the town.

The cadets were not encouraged to stray out of the college grounds but were allowed to do so under certain circumstances. The annual Croydon Fair used to provide a source of distraction but, following an incident in which some cadets (uninvited) mounted a stage to take part in a dance and a fight ensued, the fair became out of bounds. At the time it was suggested that the tone of the fair went downhill once improved public transport enabled the hoi polloi to come into Croydon!

Cadets were discouraged from frequenting pubs but, needless to say, they did. Favourites were the Black Horse, Beehive, the Far Cricketers and the King's Arms in central Croydon because of its pool table – although this venture was later abandoned for the Leslie Arms. More on pubs later. The cadets would also visit the Crystal Palace.

Numerous anecdotes exist of the lads' exploits or, as Vibart – a former cadet who recounts his fond and informative memories in *Addiscombe, Its Heroes and Men of Note* (1894) - calls it, 'ebullition of harmless fun'. We'd love to quote them all but there simply is not room. Here is just one event that occurred around 1850. As a foreword to this tale it should be noted that the cadets were not allowed out of the grounds without a letter of invitation to prove that they were going somewhere specific rather than roaming the streets and tangling with the local lads. Needless to say, some cadets used to forge letters in order to escape. For reference the reader should note that the Croydon Station is what we now know as East Croydon Station:

On one occasion a cadet having gone up to London on a fictitious invitation, chanced to meet his father in the street. The father, addressing his son by his Christian name, said, 'Why! —, what are you doing here?' The cadet's ready reply was, 'Well, old gentleman, you have the advantage of me. My name is not —, and I never had the pleasure of seeing you before.' And as he pushed past his father, he added, 'You have made a mistake. Good-bye, old gentleman, I am in a hurry.' It was early in the afternoon, and the cadet, who knew his father well, thought the latter would probably go to Addiscombe; so he turned and followed his father, who hailed a cab and got into it. The cadet did the same, and instructed the driver to follow the cab his father had entered, and when the latter arrived at the London Bridge Station, the cadet alighted from his cab and followed his father into the station. Hearing him ask for a ticket to Croydon, he also took one and travelled by the same train as his father. On their arrival, the father took a cab to Addiscombe, while the cadet ran by a short cut through the 'Wilderness' and got into his uniform just in time to meet his father's cab as it drove up to the barrack square. The father was not a little amazed to see his son and the latter simulated much surprise at his father's story. The father said he would not stay, and the son made some excuse for not accompanying his father to the station; but no sooner had the father started than the son put on his plain clothes, ran down to the Croydon Station, and again proceeded to London in the same train as his father, who never knew how he had been deceived by his son.

East front of Addiscombe House. (H.V.)

Locals of
the College Times

Mother Rose One local person was much loved by the cadets. This was Mother Rose 'for whom every cadet had a soft corner in his heart'. Her name was Dorcas Rose, and she was married to a farm labourer, John Rose. Vibart, who knew Mother Rose whilst a cadet at the college, reckoned 'To the loss of her infants (twin boys) and sweet nature may be attributed the kindly feelings she always displayed to her youthful guests and patrons'. He described her as:

... in her 48th year, a comely matron of kindly aspect who knew well how to restrain or suppress a too ardent or emphatic flow of speech. Cadets had great respect for her, and invariably supported her when she took steps to maintain discipline in her cottage.

Mother Rose's cottage was just outside the college grounds and stood on the corner of what is now Sundridge Road and Lower Addiscombe Road. At one time the cottage was denounced by the suspicious college authorities and cadets forbidden to frequent it but this order was ignored. The Lieut-Governor eventually came to the belief that it was not such a bad place after all and that 'the cottage at the north-east corner of the grounds was a better resting place for cadets than the Black Horse or Leslie Arms'.

Mother Rose would sell the cadets milk, eggs, bread and butter but no beer or 'spirituous liquors'. She used to pipe-clay the cadets' gloves.

The Roses' cottage only had two rooms, the spare room being used by cadets as a sort of club where they could chat and smoke. It was not a large room and in winter with as many as 15 to 20 cadets inside it would be thick with smoke. The walls were decorated with pictures and prints, gifts from the cadets, many of which they had drawn themselves, an ability to draw well being one of the entry requirements for would-be engineers and surveyors of the time. There were much clearer class distinctions in those days which makes the influence Mother Rose had on the cadets all the more remarkable. As Vibart commented:

That a woman of her class should have been able to retain the respect and affection of such a vast number of cadets shows in the clearest light that she was a woman of a fine nature.

When John Rose died, Mother Rose moved to St Mary's Almshouses in Wallington where she was visited by former cadets home on leave. She died there on 21 May 1894 and was buried in Beddington churchyard.

Top: *Mother Rose's Cottage (on Lower Addiscombe Road opposite Ashburton Road).* (H.V.)
Centre: *Mother Rose with cadets.* (C.L.S.L.)
Above: *The much loved Mother Rose.* (H.V.)

Paddy Another well-loved local character was Paddy (real name Fitzgibbon), who used to carry oranges, gingerbread and nuts in a tin box which he sold to the cadets. He had a wife, Biddy, who would thrash him. Cadets would occasionally encourage him to stand on a table at the Black Horse and sing songs. Once, having 'imbibed too much liquor, he became sleepy and insensible'. The cadets stowed him comfortably in a barn with straw as a bed, carried his basket and tin box away so it would not be stolen and gave them to Mother Rose for safe keeping. On recovering, Paddy was beside himself at the loss of his tin box, which was all his livelihood, and went to Mother Rose for comfort where to his great delight his property was restored.

Tarts Tarts (real name Jo Rudge) was another favourite. He ran a small shop in Croydon and was allowed to come daily to Addiscombe to set up stall under the staircase in the Fortification (or 'Slash') Hall. Tarts sold light refreshments and, while the cadets were studying, would entertain himself by playing with a small ball that he threw against the wall. Tarts had only one eye having lost the other, so he said, in a very unfair fight with a man who flung a handful of lime.

Tarts preferred to do business for cash but often gave credit. He claimed not to be able to read or write but displayed an astounding ability to maintain a running total in his head with many cadets and never hesitated to tell them the state of their score when they picked a tart from his stall. 'That', said he, 'makes 3s.5d.'

Mother Crust Mother Crust (real name Knight) was an elderly woman who sold bread and butter from a wheelbarrow near Tart's stall.

Byron Clark Byron Clark, the barber, had a small room just outside the sub-officers' room. He would cut the cadets' hair and sell cheap pomades and scents. The Addiscombe cadets were allowed to wear their hair much longer than was usual in the regular Army.

Beardie Beardie (real name Fraser) was so called on account of his long beard, very unusual at the time. He was well spoken and had the bearing of a gentleman. Beardie was believed to be well connected but lived the life of a sort of king of the beggars and referee in disputes of tramps. He had a remarkably handsome but sinister face and was said to have served as a model for an artist for the head of Christ. Cadets constantly helped him out but eventually grew tired of his scrounging and threatened that, if they found him on the college side of the boundary, they would cut off his beard.

Top: *Paddy with his basket and tin box.*
Above: *Tarts, Mother Crust and the Barber.*
(Both H.V.)

Post mutiny the British Government took over the governance of India.
This engraving depicts the Screw steamer Euphrates *in 1867.* (T.I.L.N.)

Indian reliefs embarking at Suez in 1867. (T.I.L.N.)

The Demise of The Company

The Indian Mutiny in 1857 saw the beginning of the end for the college. In 1858 the British Government took control of India from the East India Company and appointed Lord Stanley as Secretary of State for India. In 1861 the Royal and Indian Services were amalgamated, the college being then closed as of no further use. Suggestions were made to keep it going as an Army college but these were resisted by the authorities as it was considered that the existing establishments at Woolwich and Sandhurst were sufficient.

Following the Indian Mutiny, Lord Stanley addressed the cadets at the Public Examination on 10 December 1858. He spoke warmly of the cadets and the college but drew lessons from recent experiences in India pointing out how the new soldiers should conduct themselves abroad in a very accurate speech:

You cannot live, however you may attempt it, in a state of entire indifference to those who surround you in such multitudes. If you do not bear them good-will, you will bear them ill-will... A single officer who forgets that he is an officer and a gentleman, does more harm to the moral influence of his country than the men of blameless life can do good. To you therefore, in more senses than one, the honour of England in the East is committed.

And just when you thought it was all over...

The East India Company was re-established in 1987 as a result of a moment of inspiration from the present Chairman, David Hutton. A branding and marketing man by profession, he dreamt up the idea 'eureka' style while lying in the bath. He believes that in a global world of increasing confusion and information overload, recognisable brands are gaining greater significance, value and power. This led him to realise that the first, largest and most prestigious global brand remained dormant, namely The East India Company.

Antony Wild, now a Director of the company, had a similar vision quite independently. His interest and knowledge of the East India Company is now well documented in a series of authoritative books, although it was originally nurtured by his involvement in the tea and coffee trade.

As a result of their partnership the East India Company was reborn and is now a United Kingdom based public company which brings its unrivalled heritage to bear on the modern commercial world. The company trades in a wide range of goods including those historical staples, tea and coffee.

In keeping with its entrepreneurial forefathers who first set sail exactly 400 years ago, the East India Company is once again preparing itself to launch into uncharted waters, except this time the waters are virtual – the world wide web. As a company shareholder recently claimed, 'the internet is like the oceans in the great days of sail'.

When a company's success on the world wide web is largely determined by brand awareness and strength, the East India Company can launch with the confidence of knowing that it boasts vast global recognition and a trading history as the first and largest multinational the world has ever seen.

The latter-day East India Company is sensitive to the debt that it owes the East and this has served as the driving force behind the Company's internet strategy, the theme being to develop and nurture East/West and West/East trade, travel and relations on a business-to-consumer and latterly a business-to-business level. The internet venture will be run in harmony with its existing business, although the global advantages that the internet allows will help the business accelerate its long-term objectives.

In sight of its fourth centenary, the East India Company once again faces adventurous and exciting times ahead. For further information please visit www.theeastindiacompany.com

Frontispiece to Vibart's book drawn by two former cadets showing the old and new uniforms.
The Latin epitaph rues the demise of Addiscombe College and loosely translated means 'At the behest of the Queen and English Parliament, so passes the glory of the world.'

Dalmally Road. (C.L.S.L)

Sherwood Road. (B.W.)

Chapter 4
Villas Galore

by Doris Hobbs and Anne Bridge

AUCTIONS, CLEARANCE AND CONSTRUCTION: 1861-63

After the final Public Examination in June 1861 the East India College closed. The demise of the college elicited responses of both regret and opportunism. The editorial of the *Croydon Chronicle* of 16 November 1861 included the comment:

A walk in Addiscombe, Shirley and Addington... and then we stopped at the now untenanted Addiscombe, now all is silent and dull. Our thoughts went back to Henry VIII's time when it was held and owned by Heron, a London citizen of great renown...

As soon as the college closed in 1861, the ever resourceful people of Croydon began thinking up their own uses for the temporarily empty land. In July of that year the Croydon Literary and Scientific Institution announced that they were making arrangements for a Fête Champetre (country fair) to be held in August and applied to use the college grounds. Permission was refused.

Also in July 1861, the local people applied to the Croydon Board of Health for water to be supplied to the College bathing place (the Coldstream, now Academy Gardens) from the Board's works, for which they were willing to pay, in order to have a public bathing place. The Chairman, Mr William Drummond, a well-known local solicitor, gave costings and said it was practicable. However, Dr Alfred Carpenter, a member of the Board, said that he did not think that there was any chance of consent being obtained to use this bathing place. This being so, it was filled in and subsequently built over. During the days of the College, renowned for its engineering and scientific excellence, pipes had been laid to supply water from the Coldstream, somewhat earlier than Croydon Corporation who in 1851 opened the first reservoir and piped-water sewage system. The Archbishop of Canterbury switched on the pump in the Engine House in Stuart's Yard, near Surrey Street (moved from West Croydon where it had previously been used to provide power for the Atmospheric

Herons Croft, Addiscombe Road – an ancient farmhouse was rented by the Addiscombe College for one of the professors, August 2000. (S.C.)

Railway), then drove to the reservoir in Park Hill to see the arrival of the first stream of water. The water tower in Park Hill was added in 1867 to improve the water supply to the higher areas of Croydon which were then being developed (see Latham).

On 30 August 1861 by direction of the Secretary of State for India the whole of the East India Company estate, land and buildings was put up for sale by auction at the Auction Mart opposite the Bank of England. It fetched the sum of £33 600 when sold to the British Land Company. They in turn were to sell plots of land on to speculative builders.

For the following three years the estate was the scene of tremendous activity, of concurrent demolition, clearance and construction. Ashburton Road already existed as a lane on the boundary of the estate. The first new road to be marked out into building lots for sale by auction was Elgin Road, placed almost in the centre and dividing the estate into two halves. The eastern half still contained the mansion and barracks, and the western, well wooded with a great deal of standing timber and known as the Wilderness, was awaiting the sale of timber. Mr Whittingham, the auctioneer of 14 Moorgate Street, London, advertised the sale of the first portion of the estate to take place on 12 May 1862 at the Auction Mart opposite the Bank of England. It comprised 92 lots each of 20 feet frontage in the newly cut and named Elgin Road, nine slightly larger lots varying in size and three existing freehold houses fronting the Addiscombe Road, one other house on the corner of Lower Addiscombe Road and Elgin Road and the two professors' semi-detached houses on Addiscombe Road on what is now the corner of Clyde Road.

Among the stipulations of sale was, firstly, the usual one that each lot was to be fenced not exceeding six feet high and forever maintained. Secondly, there was a minimum value put on the houses (£300 to £400 each, a substantial sum for the time). Thirdly, no building was to be erected as a shop, warehouse or factory, nor any trade or manufacture carried on, nor any operative machinery to be fixed or placed on any lot. Basically, the British Land Company was ensuring that this would be an area comprising 'des res's' of some quality. No sale particulars for any other part of the estate appear to have survived but, as to this day, none of the prohibited buildings or trades are being carried on in any of the six roads – Canning, Clyde, Elgin, Havelock, Outram or Ashburton – nor on those parts of Addiscombe and Lower Addiscombe Roads bounding that area. We can assume that the same stipulations applied to the whole of that part of the estate.

Just over a month later, on 17 June 1862, at Garraways Coffee House, London, Mr Whittingham put Clyde and Canning Roads with part of Addiscombe Road up for auction. There were in excess of 118 lots but only 13 were sold on the day. The remainder and those not sold from the Elgin Road sale were then advertised for sale by private treaty. In this brand new development, would-be buyers were cautious and waited to see what sort of prices would be offered, possibly hoping that a private agreement would prove cheaper. It has been suggested that buyers wished to remain anonymous. No prices were mentioned in any advertisement nor were the names of buyers given in the auction reports.

Meanwhile, back at the College, a great deal of demolition work was taking place. The barracks, chapel and domestic buildings were the first to be destroyed, leaving the mansion and sand-modelling hall temporarily standing. The gymnasium remained in place and still stands to this day on what is now Havelock Road.

Mr Whittingham, the auctioneer, was kept busy, coming down to Addiscombe on no less than 17 occasions between 14 June 1862 and 22 August 1863. These visits were to secure the sale of reusable materials. Items offered for sale included: brickbats, firewood, over one million stock bricks, doors, window frames, floorboards, timber of all descriptions, Portland and York stone, marble chimney pieces, stone steps, water and gas piping, 100 yards of fine white sand from the sand-modelling hall and a superior turret clock complete with chiming bells. It is conceivable that some of these materials were used for the construction of the villas, as the Victorians called them, in the new roads carved into the former College grounds.

The mansion house, Havelock and Outram Roads and the western side of Ashburton Road were divided into over 215 lots and put up for auction at the Mart, Bartholomew Lane, City, on 25 May 1863. Again, relatively few lots (23) were sold on the day and the usual advertisement followed offering the remaining lots by private contract.

The mansion remaining unsold, the demolition men were speedily called in. As early as 17 June 1863 the first fittings and materials from the magnificent mansion were offered at auction: five marble mantelpieces, large black marble slabs, windows with shutters and folding doors. Features were made of the bright steel stove and the water closet with mahogany seat. A month later, on 18 July, further items came under the hammer: two oak staircases with landings, a large fossil stone chimney piece, several fine marble chimney pieces, a large meat safe, a dresser with drawers, more windows and a large number of closet pans. Perhaps the Victorians could teach us a thing or two about recycling!

Considering the old college estate was such a hive of activity, with extensive demolition and building under way, large numbers of men milling around and horse-driven carts rattling along, it is remarkable that only one reported accident appears to have occurred. This was reported in the *Croydon Chronicle* of 14 June 1862. That month a wall in the course of demolition collapsed on three of the workmen. Fortunately no one was seriously injured. Two were able to go home without assistance after treatment on the site but one, whose head was badly cut, was taken to the Union Infirmary on Duppas Hill.

The East India Company had planted around 1000 trees on the estate, largely in the area known as the Wilderness. Many of these were now felled and sold as timber, including elm, lime, oak, walnut, ash, beech, chestnut, fir, hornbeam and sycamore trees. Mercifully many escaped the axe and they, or their saplings, can be seen to this day.

There were a number of factors that made Croydon and Addiscombe an attractive prospect for potential residents and therefore developers. In 1876, after the main development in Addiscombe had taken place, Jesse Ward, owner of the *Croydon Advertiser*, observed:

Very few towns in the United Kingdom shew a greater proportionate increase in population during the past twenty years. Many reasons have conduced to make Croydon a favourite place of residence for the better class of City businessman. Its easy access to London by the frequent trains and its fame as the pioneer of sanitary reform, coupled with its natural advantages in being contiguous to some of the most lovely of the picturesque Surrey hills, have made it a popular resort when the toils of the day are over. During the decade of 1855 to 1865 the building mania prevailed to what may be called an alarming extent.

These were some of the key factors: see our sections on Latham, water/sewage, trains, coal and bricks.

A projected Addiscombe Railway Station excited a great deal of preliminary interest. You may remember that the East India Company had previously resisted the railway line entering their land. Now, however, times had changed. The *Croydon Chronicle* of 6 June 1863 carried an advertisement holding the proposed Addiscombe Station as an added inducement for the purchase of parcels of land:

Pallas (or Palace), formerly of the East India Company. (C.L.S.L.)

ADDISCOMBE COLLEGE, CROYDON, SURREY
ELIGIBLE FREEHOLD BUILDING LAND

MR WHITTINGHAM is instructed to Sell by Auction, at the Greyhound Inn, Croydon, on Tuesday, June 30th, at 6 for 7 o'clock in the Evening, A FURTHER PORTION of this ELIGIBLE ESTATE, late the property of the Hon. the East India Company, consisting of about 32 Lots of Eligible FREEHOLD BUILDING LAND, with frontages to the St. James's and Park Roads. The lots are well adapted for a good class of Villa Residences. The property is within ten minutes' walk of the New and East Croydon Station; about a mile of that of West Croydon; and when the Addiscombe Railway is completed, the station will be on the estate, thus bringing the property in constant communication with the City and West End at all times of the day. Nine-tenths of the purchase money may remain on mortgage or contract at 5 per cent, to be paid in nine years by half-yearly installments; but the whole or any part of the balance may be paid off at any time without notice.
Particulars, plans and conditions of sale may be obtained about ten days before the sale, of Mr Palace, South Lodge, Addiscombe; at the principal inns of the neighbourhood; of Messrs. Russell and Davies, 59 Coleman-street, E.C.; of the Auctioneer, 14 Moorgate Street, London, E.C.; and the place of sale.

During the 19th century the spelling of any one surname could display a certain degree of variation. It is very probable that the Mr Palace referred to in this advertisement was the same as the James Pallas who, according to the 1861 National Census, lived then at the North Lodge of the College. His wife, Ann Pallas, was lodge keeper. The picture shown here (*left*) is from the Addiscombe Photo Album, an album consisting of pictures of cadets and the college.

The Addiscombe Road Station, a terminus of the South Eastern Railway, was opened on 1 April 1864. The station was built on part of the farmland purchased by the East India Company in 1830 on the northern side of what is now Lower Addiscombe Road opposite the new Canning Road. A source of fascination and entertainment was the engine turn-table by the roadside (see map on page 12).

Local businesses of all kinds sprang up as a consequence of the new station and the new residents. The landlord of the Windmill Inn (still there on the corner of St James's Road and Lansdowne Road) advertised in the *Croydon Chronicle* of 2 April 1864, the day after the station opened, a four-stalled stable, loft, shut-up coach house and a good supply of water as being a good opening for a fly (taxi) business at the new Addiscombe Station.

This was the era of the burgeoning financial services, be it insurance or building societies. Such businesses started local advertising in the early 1860s. In 1863 the Croydon Benefit Building Society was formed, with shares at £150 each, subscriptions at six shillings a month, and entrance fee 1s.6d. per share. The Society advertised in the *Croydon Chronicle* of 7 November 1863:

This Society has been in operation for six months, has enrolled 240 members and made advances totalling £600. It is the only Society in Croydon that charges NO INTEREST on advances, and each borrower may determine the rate and time of repayment.

Such early building societies were formed for the mutual benefit of their members, that is its savers and borrowers.

It was not until the 20th century that the estate became fully developed, but the greater part of the building took place during the first decade after the sale of the first portion on 12 May 1862. The timing, facilities and location were just right! From the very beginning there was demand for the type of large

✒ Canning & Clyde Roads ✒

Left: *The bottom end of Canning Road, looking north, c.1920* (C.L.S.L.).

Below: *The top end of Canning Road, looking south, c.1910.* (J.G.)

Below left: *The top end of Canning Road, looking south, 1 January 1967.* (C.L.S.L.)

Below right: *Clyde Road, early 1900s.* (J.G.)

Below: *Top of Canning Road, looking south, 1 January 1997.* (A.B.)

Right: *Lee Villas with the former bank on the corner of Lower Addiscombe Road, August 2000.*

family house that was being built, either to buy or rent. The developers were targeting a particular, comfortably-off middle-class sector of the market who at the time were emerging as an increasingly important economic and political force. Their investment was rewarded.

So, by 1863 most of the East India Military College at Addiscombe had been swept away and replaced by six new roads lined with villas. Only five East India buildings remained, among them two houses which were demolished at the turn of the 20th century. In addition (and still standing today) there were the two professors' houses, now on the corner of Addiscombe and Clyde Roads, and the gymnasium, now converted into flats, in Havelock Road.

Clyde Road at corner of Addiscombe Road. (J.G.)

SNAPSHOT OF THE ALMOST COMPLETED DEVELOPMENT – 1871

The decade between the closure of the East India Military College in 1861 and the ten-yearly census of 1871 witnessed radical changes in Addiscombe. Housing development was rapid. By 1871 sufficient time had elapsed for a new pattern of occupation to emerge. In 1871, 173 houses were completed and occupied with a further 68 either under construction or temporarily unoccupied. In none of the roads had building been completed; some of the gaps were not filled in until the 20th century. Given the restrictions cited earlier, residential exclusivity was assured.

In addition three places of Christian worship had been built. At the southern end of Elgin Road stood the temporary church of St Mary Magdalene, Church of England, known locally as the 'tin chapel' because it was a galvanised iron hut (1868). In Canning Road was erected the large stone church of St Paul, non-conformist because the Archbishop of Canterbury refused to consecrate it (also 1868); this church still stands and is now known as the Parish Church of St Mary Magdalene (see chapter 8). In 1870 the Wesleyan Methodists built their church in Lower Addiscombe Road almost opposite the Addiscombe Road Railway Station.

CANNING ROAD

In Canning Road, as in Havelock, Outram and Ashburton Roads, the plots had a wider frontage than in Clyde and Elgin Roads. Often more than one plot was purchased in order that a larger house might be built. The houses in Canning Road were all either detached or semi-detached with the exception of 'Maitland Villas', a group of three at the north-western end, and 'Lee Villas', the nine four-storey houses immediately south of 'Maitland Villas' (of which seven remain). Lee Villas were built by the local master builder, John Woodward, who lived at No.1.

CLYDE ROAD

Clyde Road was a prime example of speculative building. The building plots were generally 20 feet wide when auctioned and this is reflected in the final development of the eastern side. These houses were of three or four storeys, often with a semi basement, and appear to have been constructed so that height compensated for the narrowness of the individual plots. There are groups of houses in terraces, in both Clyde and Elgin Roads, built to the same design by the same builder as a speculative investment on behalf of a person who had purchased a number of contiguous plots.

These terraced houses were largely constructed with two rooms on each floor, one room to the front and one facing the rear, with a single storey 'outshot' or extension at the rear on the ground level divided into two parts. The smaller part contained the water-closet and the larger part was the wash-house where a coal-fired copper was kept in which to boil the household washing and heat water when a large quantity was needed.

There were a number of different terraces in Clyde Road: Cromwell Terrace, Alexander Terrace, Clifton Terrace and Clyde Terrace. Clyde Terrace was owned by John Denton esq. who in 1869 lived at 1 Maitland Villas, Canning Road. Denton was not himself a builder but may have financed the building of the houses, possibly by Thomas Collins, a master builder of Croydon who lived at No.1 Clyde Terrace in 1869 whilst the houses were under construction. Lastly, at the south-eastern end of Clyde Road were 'Warwick Villas', a terrace of eight houses, four owned by Mr Fairfield and four by George Colliver. In 1871 neither of these gentlemen lived in the area. There were only two owner-occupied houses in Clyde Road, 'The Elms' and 'Garth Villas'. At that time, renting was far more common than today. Interestingly, both owners had bought the adjoining house as an investment.

ELGIN ROAD

Like Clyde Road, Elgin Road contained terraces: Elgin Terrace, Leamington Terrace and Frederick Terrace. Of the eight owner-occupiers, three also owned and leased the adjoining house. Athol Villas, a group of three four-floored houses with heavy stone porches, was owned by William Kennard, a draper, one of the leading shop-keepers in the town whose shops expanded and grew into one of the three most important department stores in Croydon; some may remember the donkeys outside Kennards where Littlewoods and Debenhams now stand. Kennard did not live in Elgin Road but bought the houses as an investment.

HAVELOCK ROAD

In 1871 Havelock Road was still in the early stages of its development with only nine houses completed and two of these unoccupied. Of the seven house-holders, four were owner-occupiers, a relatively high proportion for the time.

Set back from the road was the former College gymnasium which for a while had been used as the temporary church of St Paul prior to the building of the Canning Road church. A house called The Chestnuts in Havelock Road was so called after the magnificent chestnut trees that lined the approach to the North Lodge and stood opposite Chestnut Lane.

MULBERRY LANE

The former Mansion House had stood on what is now the corner of Outram Road and Mulberry Lane. On Mulberry Lane had stood Addiscombe House, residence of the College steward. Reputedly an underground passage ran from Addiscombe House to the Mansion. In the grounds of Addiscombe House had stood a great cedar which can be seen in the picture on page 20. The story goes that this was planted by Peter the Great of Russia. While he lived in England, he paid frequent visits to the Draper family. Also in the garden of Addiscombe House was a very old mulberry tree, still present in 1927. It was reputed to be one of the very earliest, if not the earliest, ever imported into England.

ADDISCOMBE ROAD

In addition to the two professors' houses that remained from the Military College, 24 more houses were erected along the stretch of road that runs between Canning and Ashburton Roads. Notable were the six ten-bedroom houses between Havelock and Outram Roads. Four of these remain and have an interesting history. At one time they formed the

Top: *Elgin Road, c.1908.* (J.G.)
Second from top: *Elgin Road, August 2000.* (S.C.)
Third from top: *Site of former Addiscombe Place/East India College on Outram Road, July 2000.* (A.B.)
Bottom: *Addiscombe Road.* (J.G.)

private Winton School which fell into disrepute and disrepair in the 1990s. Today they have been sensitively and magnificently renovated, as previously mentioned, as the Ismaili Centre.

OUTRAM ROAD

In 1871 there were 24 houses in Outram Road, all large villas generally detached but some semi-detached. Outram Villas comprised four pairs of large four-storey houses situated in the north-western part of the road.

ASHBURTON ROAD

Ashburton Road already existed as a small lane during the days of the Military College. As the eastern side of the road belonged to Lord Ashburton, it was not sold for housing until after his death early in the 20th century. On the western side 12 large houses were erected. Inhabitants included a retired jeweller, John Sulman, who owned another house in the road plus five more in Canning Road.

LOWER ADDISCOMBE ROAD

In 1871 there were 17 houses in the stretch of Lower Addiscombe Road between the Canning and Ashburton Roads. These were either large detached or four-storey pairs of semi-detached villas. 'Bernhard House', still standing on the corner of Ashburton Road, belonged to Josia Lafayette Bacon, a manufacturer of hot-water apparatus. When the house was put up for sale in 1875, a feature was the heating apparatus with marble top which heated the rooms on the ground and first floors. It is likely that this early form of central heating (1867) was an example of the heating apparatus Bacon made. (See inset piece on Bernhard house based on Daniel Wright's school project, following page).

Top: *An early photograph of Outram Road.* (J.G.)
Above: *Outram Road, August 2000.* (S.C.)
This picture: *Ashburton Road.* (J.G.)

Bernhard House, Lower Addiscombe Road

Above: *Bernhard House, July 2000.* (A.B.)

ADDISCOMBE, CROYDON.

PARTICULARS & CONDITIONS OF SALE

OF A

CAPITAL DETACHED FREEHOLD

RESIDENCE,

KNOWN AS

"BERNHARD HOUSE,"

WITH CONSERVATORY AND GARDEN;

Which will be Sold by Auction,

BY MESSRS.

BLAKE, SON, & HADDOCK,

At the Greyhound Hotel, Croydon,

On SATURDAY, the 9th day of OCTOBER, 1875,

At Four for Five o'Clock,

(Unless previously disposed of by Private Contract.)

ADDISCOMBE, CROYDON.

PARTICULARS

OF

A CAPITAL FREEHOLD

DETACHED RESIDENCE,

(Erected by a recent Proprietor for his own occupation,)

IN AN EXCELLENT SITUATION, AT THE CORNER OF THE

Ashburton Road and Lower Addiscombe Road,

On the ADDISCOMBE COLLEGE ESTATE, which is well known as one of the most healthy and desirable Residential parts of Croydon. The ASHBURTON ROAD, being the Eastern boundary of the District of ADDISCOMBE, is within easy walking distance of the

Rural Village of Shirley and the Beautiful Addington Hills,

The greater part of which latter have recently been secured by the Parish of Croydon as a Public Recreation Ground.

THE RESIDENCE IS KNOWN AS

"BERNHARD HOUSE,"

Is well built and planned, and affords the following Accommodation.

ON THE UPPER FLOOR—One Bed Room, 24-ft. by 14-ft.-6; a smaller Bed Room; Housemaid's Closet; and Door on to the Flat of Roof; Bath Room and Lavatory, with Bath and Hot & Cold Water Supply, on the Half-Landing.

ON THE FIRST FLOOR—a Bed Room, 14-ft. square; another good Room, 17-ft.-6 by 13-ft., with Balcony, and communicating with a Dressing or Bed Room, 12-ft.-9 by 10-ft.-9; a Third Bed Room; and Water Closet on the Half-landing.

ON THE GROUND FLOOR—Approached by Stone Steps from the Front Garden is Entrance Hall, with Tiled Floor, Heating Apparatus, in Ornamental Enclosure with Marble Top; this Apparatus heats the Staircase, Chamber Floor, and all the Reception Rooms.

CHEERFUL DINING ROOM, 18-ft. by 13-ft., fitted with Register Stove, and having Two Pairs of Doors opening on to a Verandah, & French Window in the Conservatory.

CAPITAL DRAWING ROOM, 22-ft. by 14-ft. (exclusive of Bay), with Register Stove and Marble Chimney Piece, and having Folding Doors to the CONSERVATORY which is heated by Hot Water, and has Steps to Garden.

LIBRARY, 12-ft.-6 by 11-ft., and Water Closet.

BASEMENT—a Breakfast Room, 18-ft. by 13-ft., with Register Stove; Pantry, well-fitted with China and other Closets, Sink, and Water Supply; Wine and Coal Cellars; Kitchen with Kitchener, Dresser, and Closets; Sculery with Copper, Sink, and Hot and Cold Water Supply; Larder; Store and Water Closets; and Tradesman's Entrance.

The House is Brick built and Slated—the exterior being Cemented on all sides—and having a dry Area round the Basement Story.

It fronts to & has a Carriage Approach with 2 Gates from the Lower Addiscombe Road;

LAWN, AND GOOD GARDEN

With well-grown and thriving Shrubs and Trees.

THE ADDISCOMBE ROAD STATION,

On the Mid-Kent Branch of the South-Eastern Railway, is within 5 Minutes' Walk of the House, from which Station there is a good Train Service to the City and Charing Cross.

To anyone engaged in London, this House should be particularly eligible, being close to a Station, near the Town of Croydon, and within an easy walking distance of a Beautiful Rural District.

The Purchaser is to pay for the Blinds, Curtains, Gas Fittings, &c., according to an Inventory to be produced, and at a sum to be named by the Auctioneers at the time of Sale. A copy of the Inventory may be seen at the Auctioneers' Offices, Croydon, and 32, Nicholas Lane, E.C., one week prior to the Auction.

The Vendor reserves the right to sell the Furniture and Effects on the Premises, at any time prior to the completion of the Purchase.

POSSESSION WILL BE GIVEN IN DECEMBER NEXT.

May be viewed by Cards, to be had of the Auctioneers.
Particulars & Conditions of Sale may be had of F. A. A. ROWLAND, Esq., Solicitor, 178, The Strand, London, W.C.; of F. GIBBONS BARNETT, Esq., Solicitor, 13, John Street, Bristol; and at the Auctioneers' Offices, Croydon, and 32, Nicholas Lane, City.

Top left and right: *Particulars and conditions of sale for the property, 9 October 1875.*

Above: *ARP Wardens were based at Bernhard House during WWII. Here they are seen at Ashburton Park.* (C.A.)

Right: *A sketch of Bernhard House by Daniel Wright aged 11.*

BERNHARD HOUSE
(Based on the school project of Daniel Wright)

The first known occupant of Bernhard House was Josia Lafayette Bacon, manufacturer of hot-water apparatus. He put the house up for auction on 9 October 1875. Daniel writes:

There was a central heating system to each room and stairway, which consisted of ornate cast iron skirting boards and vertical grills which were operated by a hot coal fire place in the basement area. Most of the rooms had a large lever to control the amount of hot air preferred in each room. Some of these features still exist but are not in operation anymore.

Between 1875 and 1933 there was a succession of occupants, including three physicians and surgeons, one of whom, Poulett Harris, lived there for 16 years between 1915 and 1931.

From 1933 to 1937 the house was occupied by W.H. Storey and Co Ltd, Wholesale Indoor Games. Daniel relates:

Over the past 20 years we have had numerous requests from people from home and abroad whose families purchased a maths game called 'Plus & Minus' from this address many years ago. They found our address on the inside lid of this game and wrote to us asking if it was possible to purchase a replacement as the game was getting too old to use (no wonder if it's more than 63 years old!).

From 1939 to 1967 there is no record of who occupied the house.

We know this house was occupied by the Army at one stage, perhaps during World War II, as the basement ceiling was reinforced against bombs and one of our bedrooms had been allocated to the 'officers'. We think the house stood empty for a number of years after the war and was then converted into two flats comprising 192a Ground Floor Flat and 192b First Floor Flat. These flats don't appear to have been occupied until 1967.

Daniel is correct. During the war 192 Lower Addiscombe Road was the Headquarters of the East ARP. Daniel's family have lived at Bernhard House since 1976. It is a beautiful house and a striking landmark in the area.

Portland Road Cycle Shop which supplied bicycles to Baldwin's butchers (see page 80). (J.G.)

THE NEW RESIDENTS - 1871

Who moved to Addiscombe as it began to grow? The 1871 national census reveals that 1063 people lived on the former East India Company land, a huge influx compared to the previous country estate and surrounding farmland and another indicator of the rapid and precise building development. How did they do it? We already know that the attractions included good transport, good sanitation, fresh air and pleasant countryside and that advertisements were aimed at the 'better class of City businessman'.

Judging by the kind of properties that had been built, the householders all enjoyed a certain level of income. Most had at least one servant. Six per cent lived on a private income. Of those who worked, many commuted into London. Twenty per cent were clerks - bank clerks, clerks at the Bank of England, solicitors' clerks, Inland Revenue men, railway audit clerks and clerks to the timber trade. Fifteen per cent worked in the professions - the Stock Exchange, the law, the Church, medicine, accountancy, and thirty-three per cent were merchants, dealers and agents - commodities traded included wine, diamonds, iron, silk, brick, oil, hops, seed and china. Nine people, four per cent, worked in shipping - there was an East India shipper, a corn lighterman, a wharfinger, two ship owners, a ship-builder and three ship brokers (the London Docks were only ten miles away and could be reached from Addiscombe or other Croydon stations). Four per cent were architects, surveyors or master builders. Six per cent were man-ufacturers - none of these had their businesses in Croydon and goods manufactured included paper collars, clothing, gold jewellery, soap, sewing machines, cork articles, brass founding, lead milling and lead pipes, hot water apparatus, accounts books and other stationery. One per cent were university students. One per cent were carpenters - these were the two carpenter's sons, aged 18 and 16, of George Alexander Bell at 'Leamington Terrace', Elgin Road. The father was a master builder so the two boys may well have been learning their father's trade.

There were twice as many women as men living on the estate but some of these were servants. Of the ladies who were not servants, only fourteen, five per cent, had a stated occupation - thirteen were teach-ers or governesses, as in Victorian times teaching was one of the few acceptable occupations for middle-class women. The other lady, Mrs Winstanley, a widow of 48 from Blackburn in Lancashire, living in Lower Addiscombe Road, was a journalist.

Not a single member of the householder families was born in Croydon. It was a truly migrant popula-tion. Nearly half had been born in London and Middlesex but some came from further afield. The connection with India was maintained by nine people who were born in the subcontinent - three in Burma and six in Bombay.

Some 268 resident servants lived on the estate; only one of them, a butler, was male. Of the 173 households, 90 per cent employed at least one servant. This compares with the national average at the time of just 6.6 per cent. Every household in Canning, Havelock and Ashburton Roads employed at least one servant. Apart from the 19 individuals born in Croydon, the servants were largely also migrants. Some households probably employed casual non-residential help for gardening, washing or other duties.

Most of the servants were young, between 15 and 29, and most were unmarried. In total 14 of the girls were aged 14 or under. Where a family retained more than one servant, the younger girls had the opportu-nity of training and being promoted in the domestic hierarchy and would have company in the kitchen when the day's work was done. But four girls aged 12, 13 and 14 years were the only servants employed in their respective household and would appear to have been maids of all work. The pay system was worked out according to both age and duties.

In 1871 no householder was living alone as sole householders were accompanied by a servant. Most people lived in households of from three to six occupants including servants.

Addiscombe's rapid expansion, especially during the 1860s, formed part of a wider picture. This was a rapidly changing era. It was the age of the railway, developments in communications, the increasingly affluent and influential middle classes, and improve-ments in health and education. Pictures of Addiscombe from the second half of the 19th and first half of the 20th century reveal a thriving local community provided for by a wide variety of shops. People had nearly everything they needed within easy walking distance.

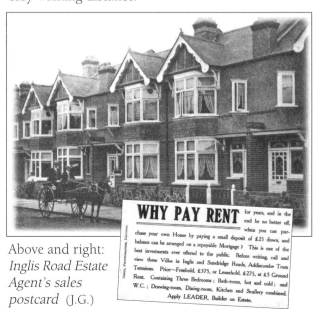

Above and right: *Inglis Road Estate Agent's sales postcard* (J.G.)

Chapter 5
Edwardian Addiscombe

by Kay Manley

In Edwardian times there began the era of the popular postcard, which could be posted and collected as many as six times a day at a cost of ½d! One can wade through pages of beautiful cards of the time, showing Addiscombe with horse-drawn vehicles, old trams, gas lighting and shops that still retained the symbols of their trade (for people who could not read). There were no less than 11 newspapers to choose from, in addition to leaflets and magazines for ladies of fashion. There were a few motor cars for those who could afford it, with a maximum speed limit of 12 mph.

Undoubtedly, the Edwardian period was in reality – for many people at least – somewhat removed from the tranquil, peaceful period it is reputed to have been. There was a very large servant class, for whom life was sheer drudgery in most cases. Although most things seem to have been very cheap compared with the present day, wages were very low also.

A middle-class community emerged in Addiscombe, however, and skilled artisans were needed, such as carpenters, plumbers, bricklayers and the like to maintain the villas. City workers found Addiscombe a convenient place to live and at the time it was recorded that 'Handsome villas spring up on every side, tenanted by city men, whose portly persons crowd the trains'. Addiscombe became synonymous with a mixture of building styles, Regency, neo-Gothic, Mock Tudor. Whereas in earlier days, pale yellow brick had been used, red brick now became far more popular.

The increase in population and concomitant number of dwellings brought the inevitable problems of drainage and sanitation (main drainage for the Lower Addiscombe Road was still being debated in 1908!). Since the inauguration of the Park Hill Reservoir there was a problem of discharge into the Coldstream which the College cadets had used for swimming, and there were many cases of typhoid and cholera as a consequence. Shop trade increased considerably with the onset of the 'tram' era. The terminus had to be at Bingham Road railway bridge in Lower Addiscombe Road, and another service came into use later, running from Crown Hill to Addiscombe Station.

Leisure areas began to appear, such as a skating rink at the top of Cherry Orchard Road (the premises later taken over by Creed & Co), motor cycling was becoming increasingly popular and in the early days of flying, displays were held not far away at Waddon. The Grant Theatre was opened in Croydon in April 1896, and there are records of theatre parties commenting on the performances there. Amateur dramatic societies began to be formed and the beginnings of the Addiscombe Drama Festival took shape. Many sporting associations were inaugurated around Addiscombe in the early 1900s, such as the Addiscombe Tradesmens' Athletic Club, long since disbanded. Addiscombe Rifle Club was founded in 1905, and the Cricket Club, founded in 1866, was still flourishing on the ground behind St Mary's in Canning Road. Billiards exhibitions drew the crowds.

All of the sports which we now accept without question were beginning to be played at weekends. Holidays were for those with money, but Sunday was play day for the ordinary Addiscombe family (with some notable exceptions). Families were able to ramble and explore the many still lovely country lanes a stone's throw away. Edwardians really appreciated fine parks and formal gardens, and it was a

The Petherick Quartet lived at 25 Havelock Road. (J.G.)

🖙 The Zeppelin Raids: Addiscombe Under Fire 🖘

Below: *The aftermath at Leslie Park Road of the zeppelin raid on 13 October 1915.* (C.A.)

Top left: *Damage at Morland Road after a zeppelin raid (see page 143).* (C.L.S.L.)

Top right: *402 Zeppelin, 1915.* (I.W.M.)

Above right: *Damage at 63 Oval Road after the raid on 13 October 1915.* (C.L.S.L.)

Above: *Damage at Edridge Road after the same raid.* (C.A.)

special treat for the children to be taken to the Crystal Palace, with its firework displays and fountains. The Addiscombe Recreation Ground was opened by the Mayoress in June 1905. Many parks had bandstands (some of which survived until after the Second World War).

The outbreak of the First World War brought the same agonies and deprivations to Addiscombe families as other districts of the time. Rolls of Honour in local churches proclaim the fact that Addiscombe men and women 'did their bit' as well as in any other borough. Bombs were dropped by zeppelin near the Leslie Arms, Oval Road School and Stretton Road, causing many deaths and injuries.

Peace came at last, and as the 1920s dawned Addiscombe was gradually becoming a continuation of Croydon, rather than a separate community, especially since the big stores were in full swing. Kennards, Allders and Grants (in that order) became very popular, and the recessions of 1928/29 were really felt more by the smaller traders in Addiscombe. It has to be noted too that the terraced type of house favoured by smaller income families which were selling at £300 were, by the 1930s, exchanging hands for more than double that amount, reflecting the financial climate of the time. Significant for the 20th

century was the speculative builder, who bought and sold individual plots with groups of Mock-Tudor, gabled and Dutch-roofed houses. Addiscombe became a mass of small houses which lined the streets with names reminiscent of the military, names such as Inglis, Warren, Hastings, Nicholson and Grant.

Top: *The Boulevard, Addiscombe Road, as you walk up from East Croydon Station.* (B.W.)
Above: *Lower Addiscombe Road showing real integrated transport with Addiscombe Station on the right and an electric tram; old Methodist Church on the left.* (J.G.)

Above: *Crystal Palace in 1898. Although Edward came to the throne in 1901, this scene would not have changed much in three years. Photograph by Emile Zola.* (N.S.)

Right: *The corner of Lower Addiscombe Road and Morland Road.* (J.G.)

Below: *The corner of Lower Addiscombe Road and Cherry*

W. CURD,
Gardener, Seedsman & Florist
73, LOWER ADDISCOMBE ROAD,
78, GEORGE STREET & LESLIE PARK ROAD, CROYDON.

Gardens tastefully Laid-Out and kept in order by contract or otherwise.
Shrubs, Plants, and Trees supplied.
Rock and Rustic Work in all designs artistically executed.

N.B.—W. CURD has recently taken the Market Garden known as the late "J. BROWNING'S Garden," Waddon.

Above: *Advertisement for Curd, 'Gardener, Seedsman & Florist'. The business offered a service laying out gardens.*

Right Girls of Addiscombe, 'Croydon Belles', pictured here in Ashburton Fields, c.1910. (J.G)

 Get your skates on!

Above: *Cherry Orchard Road and Leslie Arms.*

Left: *A poster advertising the rink at Cherry Orchard Road.*

Below: *Crowds at the new rink pose unsteadily for the camera.*
(All images this page J.G.)

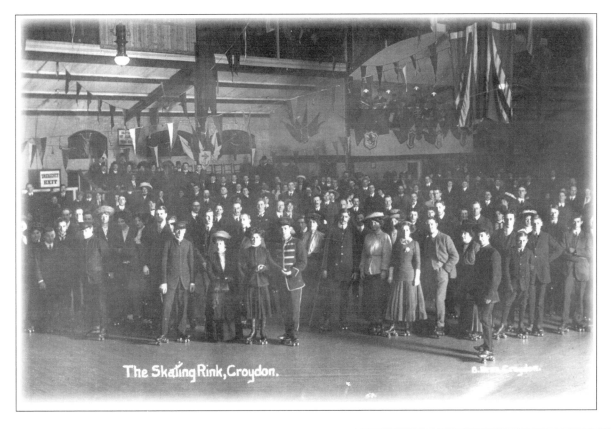

Then & Now: Lower Addiscombe Road

Top: *Lower Addiscombe Road during the Edwardian era.* (J.H.)
Above: The same view of *Lower Addiscombe Road, August 2000.* (S.C.)

❧ Then & Now: Bingham Rd Recreation Ground ☙

Top: *Entrance to Bingham Road Recreation Ground before St Mildred's was built, c.1915.* (J.G.)

Above: *Bingham Road Recreation Ground, 1918.* (J.H.)

Right: *Entrance to Bingham Road Recreation Ground, August 2000.* (S.C.)

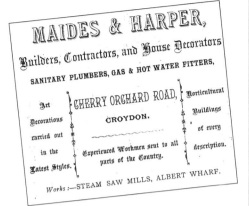

Left and above: *Site of the former brickworks, 1991. Much of the site now contains housing bounded by Northway, Davidson, Tennison and Birchanger Roads.* (D.C.)

Aerial view of Handley Brickworks, 1971. They were the largest brickworks in South London and had a huge impact on the local area. Two of their largest chimneys (there were seven in all) were 160 feet in height and constituted a local landmark visible for miles around.
In the 1930s Handley Brickworks were producing one million bricks a week! (E.H.)

Chapter 6
What a Brick!

*by Anne Bridge with thanks to Edward Handley
and Lillian Thornhill*

The mid 1800s saw an astoundingly rapid increase in housing, not only in Addiscombe and Croydon but indeed throughout the whole of London. So where did all the bricks needed for this work come from?

The area around Woodside stood on best quality London Clay, ideal for brick making. Brickworks sprung up. First to cash in on this new commercial opportunity was Thomas Mayhew, a local yeoman farmer, who in 1810 opened brickworks in a field off Dickensons Lane, where Thomas Becket School now stands, which he subsequently let to Edward Mayhew. These brickworks closed in 1856. Other brickworks included Messenger's brickworks (1838–44) on the west side of Portland Road where the Vitriol Works were later built, Murdock & Wright's brickworks (1866–74) in Alderman's Field and Hodgson's brickworks (1867–75) in Brick Meadow off Black Horse Lane.

Most significant for our area were the Handley brickworks. These first opened in Freemead in the 1880s as Horris (or Horris Parks) brickworks. In 1910 they were bought by Edward Handley and renamed Handleys. Two strata of clay existed at the site. Initially the top layer was excavated, which produced yellow London stock bricks. Examples of similar (earlier) London stocks can be seen in many of the Victorian houses in Canning Road.

The lower strata comprised blue clay. Edward Handley devised a method of baking bricks so that they burnt to red and provided excellent semi-engineering and facing bricks. The red bricks were used to build much of West Wickham, Coney Hall, Elmers End and Shirley where a strong brick was needed on the soft subsoil. The bricks were also sent as far as Southend, Eastbourne and Brighton. These hard red bricks were not always popular with bricklayers who found they were hard on even their well-worn hands.

The Handley brickworks were closed during the Second World War as bricks were not needed for obvious reasons! Edward Handley (son of Mr Handley who then owned the brickworks) remembers being on holiday with his parents in Arnside, Westmoreland, when his father received a telephone call from the Manager of the brickworks, Jack Milsted (who later became Managing Director of the company and founded the Croydon Football Club) to say that a V1 doodle bug had landed in one of the clay pits. The rocket had cut out over the brickworks and glided between two chimneys before exploding in the clay pit containing 56 million gallons of water used by the London Fire Brigade during the Blitz. Pipes ran from the clay pit to nearby roads for this purpose. There was severe damage to neighbouring Davidson Road, Beckford Road and Dickensons Lane. Fortunately no one was killed or seriously injured. The doodle bug had been launched from Holland, one of the first attacks on London.

The kilns were emptied and used for billeting Canadian soldiers, much to the delight of some of the local ladies. It was here that part of the plans for the Normandy landing were prepared. The Germans evidently marked out the brickworks as a target and dropped over 8000 incendiary bombs on them.

The Handley family lived nearby in Woodside. Edward Handley (senr) used bricks from his works to construct an air-raid shelter for his family. His son, Edward, remembers being in the shelter and hearing extraordinary noises followed by explosions. In the morning they would view the damage done by bombs. Edward Handley, meanwhile, adapted to the circumstances of the Second World War and started a successful company hiring out machines, such as excavators and dumpers, needed for clearing war-damaged sites.

After the war, bricks were again in demand. Edward Handley died in 1946 but had formed a trust by will and the trustees re-opened the brickworks. Although production never returned to the 1 million bricks per week mark, 400 000 were being produced in the 1950s and '60s providing employment for 200 men. The company was renamed the Woodside Brickworks, although the family retained control.

When the local company of Hall & Co won the contract to remove 800 000 tonnes of clay excavated during tunnelling for the construction of the Victoria tube line from Victoria to Walthamstow, Woodside Brickworks took the clay and used it to make bricks.

Hall & Co bought the Woodside Brickworks in 1963 and then sold it to Ready Mixed Concrete. Production of bricks ceased in 1974 and the buildings were pulled down. Houses were then built on part of the site. A section of the brickworks site remains today as a green area.

Alma Tavern, c.1905. (J.G.)

Black Horse and Royal Parade. (J.G.)

Chapter 7
Addiscombe Pubs

by Peter Walker

There were five major influences affecting the slow but steady growth of the Addiscombe district in the 19th century:

* The Act of Enclosure of 1800, which gave a large area of land known as Croydon Common to established land-owners in the area, enabling it to be cultivated. Over the next 50 years or so, almost all of the area was fully built up, providing much of the space needed for the expansion of Croydon.
* The Beer Acts beginning in 1830, which enabled any person with a good record to obtain a licence from the magistrates to brew and sell beer at his or her house. The object was to discourage the drinking of spirits by making beer (which was less harmful) easier and cheaper to obtain.
* The general growth in population which came about as life expectancy increased and people were able to bring up larger families.
* The break-up of the estates of land in the area as demand for building land grew.
* The convenient location of the area, close to the established town of Croydon.

With one recent exception, all of the pubs in the Addiscombe area are well over a century old; some have been rebuilt in their time, and all have been 'modernised' to some extent, and with varying degrees of success, especially towards the end of the 20th century. Addiscombe's earliest connection with pubs strikes a negative note – in 1497 John Heron, the principal land-owner in the area, had to forfeit possession of the George Hotel a mile away in Croydon, as a penalty for supporting Perkin Warbeck, the 'Great Pretender' (see Chapter 2).

Rather than deal with the individual pubs in historical sequence, we will start at East Croydon and proceed eastwards.

The Porter and Sorter (unofficially called 'Platform Seven') in Station Road was first recorded as the Station Hotel in 1869, when its clientele was almost entirely railway passengers and off-duty staff, until the new East Croydon sorting office was opened in 1968. The pub was renamed later to reflect the twofold nature of the clientele. For many years it was under threat of demolition as there were plans afoot to expand the station and/or the Post Office, but neither took place. In 1998 the property was acquired by a new company, Wizard Inns, who extensively remodelled the premises to provide much more seating and an all-day service of food.

A short distance down Cherry Orchard Road is Oval Road, which has the Oval Tavern, referred to in 1865/66 as a 'building site'. By 1869, Thomas Wilson was the licensee. For many years it retained its Victorian character, perhaps because of its location off the beaten track where it could never have been a great money-maker. In the early 1980s, after a period of closure, it was re-opened as the Sheffield Arms, a name that was soon abandoned as its fortunes revived. Later in the decade it grew in popularity and was enlarged to accommodate increasing business. Food is provided at lunchtime and in the evenings, with jumbo pizzas being a speciality.

Returning to Cherry Orchard Road is Oval Road and turning round the bend on the right is the site of the Nags Head at No.78 Cherry Orchard Road. This pub was opened in 1851 by George King, and it continued in business until 1930, the premises being entered in the 1939 directory as a 'fishing tackle

Station Hotel, opened 1869.
This is now the Porter and Sorter.
(J.G.)

shop'. The building was demolished after the Second World War.

A short distance along on the left hand side at the corner of Cross Road is the Grouse and Claret, a pub with an unspoiled exterior, opened as the Horse and Groom in about 1832 when Stephen Rose was the first licensee. It was renamed in the 1980s and in its new image it has acquired a reputation for jazz and good food.

A forgotten pub building which still stands is the old North Pole at No.43 Cross Road, which appeared as the Fox and Hounds in the 1845 rate book, soon to be renamed the North Pole, under which title it traded until the early 1900s. In the late 1990s the building was used as a motorcycle accessory shop.

Returning to Cherry Orchard Road, the Cherry Orchard appeared in directories for the first time in 1855 as a beer-house run by John Howard. It is the only pub in this area to have been rebuilt in the 20th century, in the 1920s, and it survives in this form although the name was shortened to Orchard.

The 1855 directory refers to buildings on the north corner of Cherry Orchard Road and Leslie Park Road as 'new houses erecting'. Two years later the corner building was occupied by James Davies, a beer retailer. This later became a fully licensed pub known as the Surrey Arms which continued in business until 1928, when it was pulled down with the adjoining properties and rebuilt as a new parade of shops which still bears the building date, 1929.

Further along Cherry Orchard Road, at the crossing with Lower Addiscombe Road, is the Leslie Arms, opened in 1851 as a beer-shop owned by Croydon brewers, Nalder and Collyer, and run initially by Edward Bellamy. It was originally a free-standing building with a yard fronting on to Cherry Orchard Road, but it was built, together with a matching parade of shops, in the 1880s, to become a major landmark in the area.

Retracing our steps along Cherry Orchard Road and turning into Leslie Park Road, we see the Builders Arms, originally a beer-house which opened in 1864/65 with William Coombes as proprietor. It survived almost untouched until the 1970s, since which time it has been steadily and successfully enlarged and modernised, and now serves quality beers and lunchtime and evening meals.

Leslie Park Road leads to Lower Addiscombe Road and the Alma is about 200 yards further east. The site on the corner was acquired by the Croydon brewers, Nalder and Collyer, in 1864. According to that company's records, the Alma public house was built in that year but there is no mention of the public house in the 1865/66 *Croydon Directory* and it is not until the 1869 edition that the name of the licensee, Robert White, is given. Eliza Ann Dallman held the pub by the time of the next issue of the

Top: *The largest pub clock extant in Croydon pictured here in the Alma. Former landlord, Bill Webb, pioneered late opening until 10.30p.m.* Above: *Leslie Arms, August 2000.* (S.C.)

guide in 1874 and she remained there until at least 1878. By 1889 James Blake had taken over, to remain for five years, followed by D. Gowenlock from 1885 to 1888 and A. Woodhouse from 1890 until 1897. In recent years the Alma has been refurbished and extended into a neighbouring shop and some remarkable Victorian bar fittings have been installed.

There is one other pub in the western portion of our area, the Cricketers at No.107 Addiscombe Road, which opened as a beer-house in 1874 with William Flowers as licensee. The building was one of a series of cottages along Addiscombe Road and it is probably the same one which had been the Queen beer-house, opened by 1843 by John Cotton and leased from Henry Bance – the rateable value of this property in 1844 was a mere £10, whereas the older Black Horse (see below) was worth the princely sum of £19.10! The Queen ceased trading in 1853/54 and there were apparently no licensed premises in the immediate vicinity for about 20 years.

Half a mile to the east is the Claret Free House, Bingham Corner, which has already been mentioned. A shop unit was converted into a wine bar in the 1980s, trading as the Claret Wine Bar. In practice it was found that beer was selling better than wine and so after ten years the premises were renamed to reflect the nature of the business. Despite its short life as a bar, it has a great pub atmosphere.

The oldest pub in the area is the Black Horse, at 335 Lower Addiscombe Road, which may date back to the 16th century. It was acquired in the 18th century by Robert and Charles Smith, brewers of Croydon, whose business had been founded back in the late 1500s. Towards the end of the 18th century, the Smith family must have exceeded themselves in building up the brewery and an estate of pubs, and in 1798 they sold their impressive brewery in Croydon High Street, together with ten of their pubs in the vicinity which included the Black Horse.

The 1811 census records two victuallers in the Addiscombe-Shirley area, a Richard Meager, with two other males and two females in his family, and a William Meager. One of these would have been at the Black Horse, while the other would have been at the old Shirley Inn over a mile away. It was not until later Victorian times that the pub had any neighbours: Roberts' map of 1847 shows the Black Horse, Woodside and its outhouses standing alone at the corner of the lane to Woodside, now known as Black Horse Lane. The immediate area did not much benefit from the opening of the Addiscombe Railway Station half a mile away (opened in 1864) or Bingham Road Halt a quarter of a mile away (opened with a very spasmodic service in the 1890s). However, it did receive a horse tram route as early as 1883 running between George Street, Croydon and Portland Road near Norwood Junction Station. Running as it did through largely undeveloped land, the tramway did not flourish except on race days at the Woodside Race Course and, when the course closed in 1894, it was cut back to the Alma in Lower Addiscombe Road. From then onwards, just as the area was being built up, the bus was the only mode of public transport.

The other pub which bears the name 'Cricketers' in the area, in Shirley Road, dates back to the mid 1880s. A cluster of small cottages had been built early in the century and by 1851 one of them had become a beer-house run by Samuel Bucknall.

PUBS IN ADDISCOMBE: 17TH CENTURY TO 2000

Name (alphabetical)	Address	Earliest date	Latest
Alma	129 Lower Addiscombe Road	1864	(open)
Black Horse	335 Lower Addiscombe Road	17th century?	(open)
Builders Arms	65 Leslie Park Road	1865	(open)
Cherry Orchard (later Orchard)	112 Cherry Orchard Road	1855	1980s
Claret Free House (ex wine bar)	5a Bingham Corner	1990s	(open)
Claret Wine Bar (later free house)	5a Bingham Corner	1980s	1990s
Cricketers (ex Queen)	107 Addiscombe Road	1874	(open)
Cricketers	157 Shirley Road	1851	(open)
Fox and Hounds (later North Pole)	43 Cross Road	1851	1855
Grouse & Claret (ex Horse & Groom)	83 Cherry Orchard Road	1980s	(open)
Horse & Groom (later Grouse & Claret)	83 Cherry Orchard Road	1832	1980s
Leslie Arms	Lower Addiscombe Road	1853	(open)
Nags Head	78 Cherry Orchard Road	1851	1930
North Pole (ex Fox and Hounds)	43 Cross Road	1859	1900
Orchard (ex Cherry Orchard)	112 Cherry Orchard Road	1980s	(open)
Oval	131 Oval Road	1855	(open)
Porter and Sorter (ex Station Hotel)	Station Road	1980s	(open)
Queen (later Cricketers)	107 Addiscombe Road	1843	1853
Station Hotel (later Porter and Sorter)	Station Road	1869	1980s

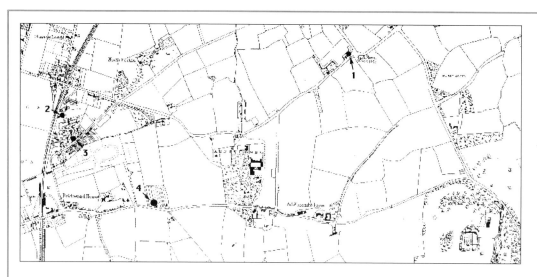

1847

1. Black Horse
2. Fox &
   Hounds
3. Horse &
   Broom
4. Queen

1868

1. Black Horse
2. Builders
   Arms
3. Cherry
   Orchard
4. Cricketers,
5. Horse &
   Groom
6. Leslie Arms
7. Nags Head
8. North Pole
9. Surrey Arms

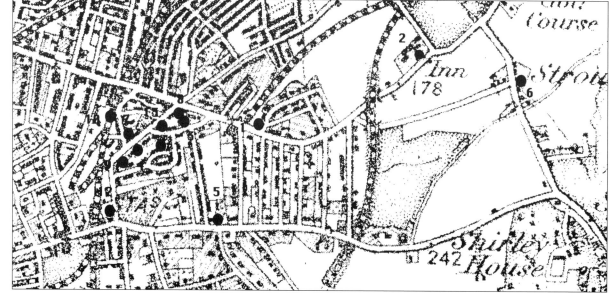

1874

1. Alma	2. Black Horse	3. Builders Arms	4. Cherry Orchard
5. Cricketers (107 Addiscombe Road)		6. Cricketers (Stroud Green Road)	
7. Horse & Groom	8. Leslie Arms	9. Nags Head	10. North Pole
11. Oval	12. Station Hotel	13. Surrey Arms	

Chapter 8
Churches of the Borough

by Anne Bridge and Revd Charles Budden

St Mary Magdalene

The strangely beautiful church of St Mary Magdalene stands solidly in Canning Road. Its eccentric appearance seems, curiously, to give it a character and life of its own. Just a little research reveals that its beginnings were as bizarre as its appearance.

Rebellion, rivalry, resentment – all marked the early days of the local church and provided fodder for the local press.

As the land formerly occupied by the East India Company was rapidly covered with houses, so the population of the area grew apace. Churchgoers in England at the time were largely Church of England. By 1866 some of the new people had decided that St James' Church was too far away and moved to form a new congregation in Addiscombe. They rather took matters into their own hands. The newly opened St Matthew's (1866) enjoyed the ministrations of a talented young curate by the name of Ben Oliel.

Ben Oliel possessed a brilliant intellect and could attract great crowds with his rousing preaching. A number of Addiscombe dwellers decided to secure his services for their proposed church. They duly approached the Vicar of St James' and suggested that he should appoint Ben Oliel as Curate-in-Charge of a new district of Addiscombe. The Vicar of St James', however, repeatedly refused to consider it.

Not to be deterred, the people of Addiscombe simply declared UDI and poached Ben Oliel who left St Matthew's at the end of August 1866. This was an extraordinary situation. Ben Oliel and his supporters bought Havelock Hall (the former gymnasium of the East India Company that still stands in Havelock Road) and opened it as St Paul's Church on Sunday 20 January 1867. As this was not an official Church of England church, it was not consecrated.

So great was the success of St Paul's, however, that further accommodation was sought. Ben Oliel's wealthy brother-in-law, Robert Parnell, who lived in Cornwall House, Addiscombe Road, agreed to pay for a new church and gave Ben Oliel a free hand in seeking an architect. Edward Buckton Lamb was chosen. He was a highly original architect not always favourably viewed by other Victorian Gothic architects. The flame shape that can be seen in the windows was one of his favourite motifs. Sadly he died bankrupt before the church was completed.

The foundation stone of the church was laid on 3 June 1867 and on 29 September 1868 the church opened at 12 noon. The offerings at that service (£50) were donated to the fund for building Croydon General Hospital. Not having the sanction of the official church, the new St Paul's was still not consecrated. Nor was the building complete as they had run out of money. The church was originally designed to have an impressively tall spire. This never materialised in its original design and for 60 odd years what is now the tower stopped just above the door. Even to this day the Kentish flagstones that can be seen at the front of the church do not cover the back of the church which is plain brick.

Meanwhile, however, the Archbishop and Vicar of St James' had conspired to set up a 'lawful' church on the same patch. They formed a new district and appointed the Revd Morse as clergyman. On 6 August 1868 the new Iron Church was opened at the top of Elgin Road and given the name of St Mary Magdalene. Rivalry ensued.

All was going well for St Paul's until one Sunday Ben Oliel sprung a surprise on his congregation. At that time in the Church of England there was a good deal of antagonism between the evangelical brigade (or Low Church) and the ritualistic brigade (or High Church). The fiery preaching of Ben Oliel had well suited the evangelical brigade who had started up St Paul's with him. Suddenly, on 30 June 1872, he jumped ship and went ritualistic. Half of his congregation promptly upped and left to join the rival St Mary Magdalene. The numbers at St Paul's declined until the church was closed in December 1873.

The magnificent building stood as a sad, empty shell for the best part of two years. During this time bitter wrangling raged between Ben Oliel, who had bought the freehold from his brother-in-law, and the Church of England authorities who wished to purchase the building, since their own accommodation was now bursting at the seams with the combined congregations of St Mary Magdalene and

St Mary Magdalene and Vicarage. (J.G.)

St Mary Magdalene, c.1905, minus the tower. (J.G.)

the former St Paul's. Needless to say, Ben Oliel was asking for a far higher price than the Church was prepared to pay.

Eventually an agreement was reached, whereby the congregation offered subscriptions to begin paying for the building, and the church in Canning Road formally re-opened as St Mary Magdalene on 5 August 1874. Mind you, the Bishop refused to consecrate it until Wednesday 31 July 1878 – for only by then had the people of Addiscombe finished paying their debt.

This concluded a highly embarrassing few years that had attracted the attention of the local press. It must have been with some relief that the Addiscombe Church Committee, shortly before the re-opening, read in the *Croydon Advertiser* of Saturday 18 July 1874 the following words :

We lay before our readers of to-day a piece of news which we think must be particularly gratifying. The Addiscombe Church Difficulty is at an end. A district which has long been vexed by unseemly disputes in religious matters, and which has had no adequate church that could be called its own, is now in possession of a beautiful edifice in which the orthodox services of the Church of England will hereafter be held.

Main picture: *St Mary Magdalene complete with its tower which was built in October 1928.* (A.B.)
Inset: *Ben Oliel.* (C.L.S.L.)

The foundation stones of St Mildred's church and chapel are laid, 1931. (S.M.R.B.)

Consecration of the church, 9 October 1932;
procession of the Witness with Mr H.G. Williams MP. (S.M.R.B.)

St Mildred's Church

In such manner dreams can be made to come true quickly.   Charles D. Budden, 1937

The Birth of a Parish   When the Church of St Mary Magdalene, in Canning Road, was consecrated in the year 1878, the entire population of Addiscombe probably did not exceed 2000. At that time our own parish was parkland forming part of the Ashburton manorial estates.

In the year 1912 some 350 houses had been erected on this estate, and as there was no place of worship of any kind nearer than St Mary Magdalene, the Church of England Men's Society' met under the leadership of Mr A.E. Crook, renting a small building known as the Gordon Hall for a year. The Revd Thomas Bentham MA was appointed by the Vicar of St Mary Magdalene (the Revd Henry Glover) as Curate-in-Charge. The venture was successful, and the need for a more permanent place of worship became so strongly felt that a committee was formed and a fund instituted for raising money to provide a proper Chapel of Ease.

The new church was opened for worship in 1914. In these early days the district was very different from that which has become familiar to us today. Bingham Road was but a lane, and in wet weather those who attended church were forced to walk on planks to get there dryshod.

Then came the tragic days of the First World War. At 12 o'clock each day the church bell (which we still possess) was rung as a reminder to the parishioners to offer special prayers for the men who were at the Front, and in the early part of 1918 Evensong was held at 4 o'clock on Sunday afternoon so that the congregation might get home before the air raid started. And when the conflict was over, a Thanksgiving for Peace was inaugurated and the money collected used to purchase the freehold ground on which the present church buildings stand. That was a far-sighted act. Without the

land the great programme of 1931 to 1937 could not have been carried out.

The absence of a suitable hall for week-day activities being keenly felt, the next step was to inaugurate a fund for that purpose. This hall is now known as the St Mildred Small Hall (1921). The next year (1922) marked another milestone in the progress of the church and the development of the parish. The area was cut off from St Mary Magdalene. The actual (parish) boundary is in the middle of the railway line. Passengers therefore travel from London in the parish of St Mildred but going to London are in the parishes of St Mary Magdalene, Addiscombe, and St Luke, Woodside. Finally on 5 August, Mr Bentham was licensed as the 'Minister of the Peel District of St Mildred, Addiscombe'. So ended the first decade.

The year 1923 saw the formation of the first Parochial Church Council, whose main task henceforth was to further the Building Fund and provide the district with a permanent church and with a Parsonage House. Already the population had reached 7000. The bazaar in that year made £259, which included the curious item 'Sale of Dog, £1'.

The year 1928 is described as 'full of lights and shadows' and the loss of Mr Thomas's services as curate was keenly felt. Mr Bentham was then beginning to feel the pressure of all the past work, having already passed the allotted span of three score years and ten. But the hopes of the congregation still ran high. The Parochial Church Council then accepted plans by Mr Hare for a new church, and a tender for part of the work amounting to £16 155 was provisionally accepted. Alas, this optimism was not justified. Although the year 1929 opened with every sign of increasing prosperity, it ended in the minor key. The plans for building had to be abandoned. Age had taken its toll and early in 1931 Mr Bentham resigned the living. He was then 75 years old and his strength was spent. But he had planted well and God was soon to give the increase and also permit His faithful servant to see the fruits of his labour.

Consecration of the church, 9 October 1932; procession of the Makers of Music. (S.M.R.B.)

❧ Building of St Mildred's ❧

Above: *Revd Charles Budden.*

Top right: *The 'mad vicar', Revd Charles Budden, examines plans for the church, 1931.*

Right: *Cutting the first sod, 1931.*

ST. MARY MAGDALENE CHAPEL OF EASE.

Garden Fete

IN AID OF THE
CHURCH BUILDING FUND

GORDON HALL and GROUNDS

Children! Look out for the SWEET STALL and the SWINGS.

June is the month for FLOWERS. At the Flower Stall you will be well and cheaply Supplied.

Programme.

3.10	....	Children's Country Dance
3.20	....	Orchestra (in the Hall)
3.45	....	Concert (in the Hall)
4.15	....	Demonstration of First Aid by St. Mary's Troop of Boy Scouts.
4.30	....	Children's Dance
4.40	....	Orchestra
5.0	....	Concert
5.30	....	First Aid Demonstration
5.45	....	Children's Dance
6.0	....	Orchestra
6.30	....	Concert
7.0	....	Orchestra

During the Afternoon and Evening Visitors will find various Amusements in the Grounds, including Houp-la, Cocoanut Shy, Swings for Children, Competitions, Egg and Spoon Races, etc.

Don't fail to visit the *FANCY STALL* in the Gordon Hall. There is something for Everyone.

TEAS & LIGHT REFRESHMENTS AT POPULAR PRICES. Strawberries & Cream. Vanilla Ices

PRICE ONE PENNY.

Left: *Garden Party, 1931.*

Above: *Cutting the first sod choir procession, 1931.* (All images on this page S.M.R.B.)

THE BUILDING ST MILDRED'S
by Revd Charles Budden

In 1931 the district was under the guardianship of the two churchwardens until the day arrived, 24 April, when I was instituted by the Bishop of Croydon and licensed as 'Minister of the Peel District of St Mildred, Addiscombe.'

I confess that my heart sank when I first entered the little temporary church in Bingham Road. The Church Hall, too, seemed bleak and dreary. But these feelings of dismay vanished under the warmth and cordiality of our reception. I felt the sense of promise that the task to which I had set my hand would be fulfilled.

We fixed 12 June for a big Parochial meeting, at which the Bishop of Croydon was to be present and our building programme formulated. It was enthusiastically attended and the Bishop spoke in his usual cheering way: 'You mean to go full steam ahead,' he said, 'and I have no doubt you will succeed. When you have got a stiff job to do, it is no good going about grousing and growling and being afraid of it. So many people have the 'no' complex and say 'It can't be done,' but the stiffer the job the happier you ought to be.' In a talk with me afterwards he put it even more strongly: 'The bold course is the only safe course,' and on that we acted.

So the die was cast, and the plans for the present church and vicarage designed by the late Cecil Greenwood Hare, FRIBA, were passed. It was an adventurous undertaking. True, we had assets to the value of £6000, but none of those assets were to materialise until building began and some not until it was completed. Our immediate cash balance was somewhere in the region of £2000 and with that slender capital, and in the faith that the money would be forthcoming, we signed a contract with Messrs Down Bros of London for £28 147. People in those days spoke of the 'mad Vicar of St Mildred's.'

The dedication of the site and the cutting of the first sod the day before the builders began was an historic occasion. But how it rained! The rain did not damp our spirits. We were keyed up with excitement. Led by the Processional Cross, the choir paid no heed to their soaking surplices, but nobly processed down Bingham Road singing the great hymn 'Pioneers' from 'Songs of Praise'. The congregation carried shovels, spades, trowels and any other cutting instrument, joined in lustily by a brass band very much out of time and tune! And then we manned the site and Mr Bentham, taking a new

Revd Thomas Bentham of St Mildred's 1912–31. (S.M.R.B.)

bright spade, cut the first sod on the place now occupied by the altar. It was a great day.

The foundation stone of the New Church was laid by the Archbishop of Canterbury (the Most Revd Cosmo Gordon Lang) on Friday afternoon, 9 October, in warm sunshine. Indeed, it was fortunate that the day was so fine, for the ceremony was delayed quite half an hour as the Bishop of Croydon's robes went astray, the Sacristan mistaking the time. I shall never forget that half-hour as the Archbishop waited with us in the confines of the tiny vestry of the temporary church. The reason for the smallness of the vestry was quaint and may be here stated: it appears that when the architect designed the church he forgot to leave a place for the organ – so the organ was put in the Minister's vestry. A more inconvenient arrangement has yet to be discovered. Believe me, the conversation was not in decorous whispers when the organ was being played. However, on this historic occasion it was only the cramped space we suffered from. I tried at the end of the first quarter of an hour nervously to pour oil on troubled waters. 'We are only fifteen minutes late, Your Grace,' but wilted instantly under the reply: 'Only fifteen minutes.'

The foundation stone which is now embedded in the north-east tower pier is a fragment of Canterbury Cathedral and came from that part of the east end, known as 'Becket's Corona' because below it was a shrine containing a portion of Becket's scalp. We were particularly favoured in securing this stone from the Dean and Chapter of the Cathedral as it is their rule only to give such stones to churches of cathedral rank. But I had been preaching in Canterbury Cathedral and used the opportunity for pressing our request. We devised all sorts of ways for raising funds, one of which was destined to be a lead to the rest of the country, namely, an offering of jewellery. A Sunday was set aside for this, and the people brought their rings, their bracelets, their chains, their old watches, and many other pieces and even bits of jewellery of gold and silver which, when melted down, totalled nearly £80. Not long afterwards, our country was involved in the terrible financial crisis of the fall of 1931. England went off the gold standard and the stability of our whole banking system was for a moment questioned. The price of gold leapt upwards and throughout the land the people turned their jewellery into cash. We had only just been in time.

The year 1932 opened in a welter of conflicting emotions. We oscillated between hopes and fears.

St Mildred's in 1932 before the tower was built. (S.M.R.B.)

St Mildred's in 1933. (S.M.R.B.)

My greatest fear was lest anyone should ever find out that I was afraid! We had taken the precaution in our building contract to provide a clause whereby building could be stopped without penalty if we found ourselves unable to raise the money for the required installments which had to be paid as the work progressed.

We decided to postpone the building of the tower and chapel, but even so we were faced with the problem of finding immediately the sum of £9000 to meet the contractors' bills. We arranged for an overdraft at the Westminster Bank for £10 000. In this matter Mr Walter Smith, the Manager of the Addiscombe Branch of the Westminster Bank and Hon. Treasurer of our Building Fund, proved a stout friend and persuaded his Directors that the money could be safely loaned to us.

Yet the financial crisis (in the country) was our salvation. We were perhaps the only church in the Diocese willing to build at that time, and so, as it were, we got in first. We also enjoyed the advantages of unprecedentedly low costs.

On 1 February we moved into our new Vicarage. A feature of the house is that over every doorway is affixed an oak name-plate inscribed in red and black with the names of St Mildred's kinswomen who were canonised. The list is as follows: Dining-room, St Domneva; Drawing-room, St Eanswith; Library, St Werburga; Kitchen, St Ebba; Bedrooms, Saints Etheldreda, Hilda, Lioba, Sidwell, Zitha and Frideswide. On the outside of the house is a stone house plate over the front door inscribed with the letter 'M' and a lamp – St Mildred's emblem. The doorknocker is a conventional 'head' representing our patron saint.

At the end of April we owed the Bank a full £10 000. It was an anxious time. Our architect, Mr Cecil Greenwood Hare, FRIBA, died on 14 July, and for some time I functioned in his place. I little thought when in 1925 I took a degree in architecture, purely as a hobby, that the time would come when the technical knowledge thus acquired would be of practical use. But it fitted in with so many other things, that I never had any conviction in my life so strong as that God had sent me to do this work.

On Saturday 9 October, the new church was

Above: *Revd and Mrs Budden.* (S.M.R.B.)
Bottom: *One of the fund-raising events, 11 May 1932.*

consecrated by the Archbishop; the Peel District of St Mildred became a parish and I was advanced from the position of 'Minister' to that of 'Vicar'. It was a great day and one that can never be equalled in our parochial history. It was given enormous publicity. Accounts of the ceremony, many of which were illustrated, were published in every leading newspaper of the United Kingdom and the news even penetrated into many of the Continental papers.

The service was an ambitious one, but it went off without a hitch. It was divided into several sections, the first being 'The Service of Transit' when six processions converged upon the new church in order: first, the procession of the makers of music, then the Parochial procession, next the procession of witness; fourthly, the procession of the Mother Church of St Mary; after that, the procession of pastors; and lastly, the mayoral procession. All these had to be carefully timed so that those coming from the old church did not collide with those entering from the new vestries. In the procession of the makers of music, which was the ceremonial designation for the choir, the Litany was sung and as it was very essential that this should end at exactly the right moment, the Revd Cyril J. Lee (then our curate) and myself rehearsed it carefully the day before to the astonishment of the passers-by who could only surmise that two clergymen, one at any rate old enough to know better, had apparently gone off their heads.

To say we were blessed with very fine weather for the afternoon after a morning which seemed to augur certain disaster to our programme is to speak literal truth. So black was the outlook at two o'clock that I decided that we could not have any outdoor processions, but at a quarter-past two the sky lifted and at half-past two, when the first procession was due to start, the rain ceased and did not recur. And then the way the sun suddenly illuminated the building as the Archbishop signed the Deed of Consecration was quite dramatic and would in bygone days have been declared a miracle.

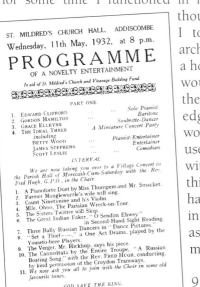

ST. MILDRED'S CHURCH HALL, ADDISCOMBE
Wednesday, 11th May, 1932, at 8 p.m.

PROGRAMME
OF A NOVELTY ENTERTAINMENT

In aid of St. Mildred's Church and Vicarage Building Fund.

PART ONE

1.	EDWARD CLIFFORD	Solo Pianist
2.	GORDON HAMILTON	Baritone
3.	GRACE ELLEYNE	Soubrette-Dancer
4.	THE IDEAL THREE	A Miniature Concert Party
	including	
	BETTY WOOD	Pianist-Entertainer
	JAMES STEPHENS	Entertainer
	SCOTT LESLIE	Comedian

INTERVAL

We are now taking you over to a Village Concert in the Parish Hall of Morecash-Cum-Saturday with the Rev. Fred Hugh, G.P.O., in the Chair.

1. A Pianoforte Duet by Miss Thumpem and Mr. Smacket.
2. Farmer Manglewurzle's wife will sing.
3. Count Nimetynnine and his Violin.
4. Mlle. Obno, The Parisian Wreck-on-Tour.
5. The Sisters Twitter will Skip.
6. The Great Indian Faker, " O Sendim Ehwey " in Second-Hand Sight Reading.
7. Three Bally Russian Dancers in " Dance Pictures."
8. " Set a Thief——," a One Act Drama, played by the Youseti-bece Players.
9. The Verger, Mr. Hickhup, says his piece.
10. The Cannedtata by the Entire Troupe, " A Russian Boating Song," with the Rev. FRED HUGH, conducting, by kind permission of the Croydon Tramways.
11. We now ask you all to join with the Choir in some old favourite tunes.

GOD SAVE THE KING.

35

The year 1933 opened with our proud possession of a consecrated church, though that church consisted only of a nave. It was in fact far from beautiful and the east end on the outside was a hideous eye-sore. I was criticised severely for building in this way. What we should have done, said the detractors, was to have built the Chancel first. In the May issue of our monthly *Magazine* the ball was started rolling once again. I said:

There are, indeed, four good reasons why we should go forward: 1. Because, if we do not go forward, we shall stop. 2. Secondly, we owe it to the unemployed to provide work which new building entails. 3. We ought to build because we can do it. 4. We should rebuild as a gesture of confidence in God and in ourselves. The world today is paralysed by fear. Fear is the deadliest enemy of progress.

The museum had already been started. We had sold the temporary church to a body of Nonconformist friends called 'The Open Brethren'. We had also built a fine tennis pavilion and laid down two hard courts. In such manner dreams can be made to come true quickly.

On October 7 the foundation stone laid by the Archbishop was unveiled by the Bishop of Croydon and three memorial stones laid in the remaining piers of the tower. The first was a 15th-century fragment of the Parish Church of Croydon; the second was a stone from St Mary Magdalene's church, Addiscombe; and the third the foundation stone of the temporary Church of St Mildred. This stone was appropriately laid by Mr Bentham. Thus our tower and sanctuary stand four-square upon the past and the genealogical history of our church is incorporated into its fabric.

The laying of these stones awoke great interest and again we enjoyed tremendous publicity, not the least advantageous being the filming of the ceremony and its exhibition at the Davis Theatre, Croydon.

The following year opened with a tremendous thrill. At the Twelfth Night Carnival, the announcement was made that the next morning, during Mattins, a great piece of news was to be told.

It is needless to say that a large congregation gathered expectantly and listened impatiently to the usual long list of notices and then at last the great moment came:

Last night, through the amazing generosity of Mr and Mr J.H. Parker of 58 Northampton Road, we were presented with a cheque for five thousand pounds, for the purposes of erecting a new Parish Hall.

It is impossible to describe the thrill that went through the congregation at this good news. But as events proved we were not to build the new hall quite as soon as we had hoped. It was found that the site could not be cleared until the following year and so with Mr Parker's consent the money was allowed to lie at the Westminster Bank against our Building Fund overdraft. This was an enormous financial relief.

Then came the next milestone, the consecration of our new Sanctuary on Saturday 21 April. The first celebration of Holy Communion in the new Sanctuary took place on Sunday, 22 April, at 8.15a.m., when the celebrant was the Revd Thomas Bentham.

A feature of the new Sanctuary is the Rood Beam surmounted by a large wooden cross. Within the beam a canvas lantern sheet is fixed, operated by a concealed winch on the outer side of the north-west tower pier.

We had by that time established the use and proved the value of the lantern in church for illustrating sermon, service, or lesson, as the case may be. It was a venture that met at first with violent opposition from some quarters.

In 1935 the great Million Pennies Scheme got underway. The credit for this must be given to Mr S.H. Allen. It was ambitious but it proved effective. The aim was to reach one million pennies in 12 months, that is, the substantial sum of over £4000. It seemed impossible and perhaps it was impossible, but we nearly did it. Actually the amount was reached in 22 months. It included grants from the Archbishop's New Churches Fund of £1700.

The merit of the scheme rested upon the appeal it made to the humblest effort. I wrote in our *Magazine*:

Yes, a penny is a small thing but so is a drop. A brick is a small thing, but our church is built of bricks – each one of which was laid individually. Mere size is nothing.

The new hall was opened on Saturday, 5 October by Mr and Mrs John Parker. In the evening a great Celebrity Concert was held, again the gift of Mr Parker. A unique array of talent was presented. How the New Hall has furthered the work is now common knowledge. It is no exaggeration to say that through it we were enabled to finish the building of the church, for not only did it permit us to hold those many and varied functions by which we raised the necessary funds, but it provided accommodation for the social and religious organisation of the parish on which its life and growth depend.

A very notable addition to the Museum had been a fine assortment of Egyptian antiquities presented by the Trustees of the British Museum; a collection of over 2000 fossils giving a complete sequence of the geological history of the world; a number of valuable relics from Ur; and a unique series of thousands of the world's sea-shells.

The completion of the church, 1936-37

In the March issue of the *Magazine* I wrote:

A Chapel is sorely needed for the smaller services. It is essential when building a church in stages, as we have done, that no stage should be indefinitely postponed. The momentum must be kept up.

We did no building in 1936. The New Year opened with a change in the Building Fund secretaryship. For ten years Mr S.H. Allen had been Hon. Secretary of our Church Building Fund, of which he had been the mainstay. The spirit alike provides the driving force and creates the goodwill without which no concern can prosper; and although we all feel it, the effect of that cheerful, optimistic, willing spirit which has characterised Mr Allen lives on.

Work on the new building began in May 1937 so that the final dedication would be on 9 October of that year, when the Archbishop of Canterbury would pay his fourth visit to the parish - four visits in five years! Surely that is another record.

While we were building, news came of the sudden death of my predecessor, the Revd Thomas Bentham MA. A pioneer is one who makes history, and such a one was Mr Bentham. His work was essentially the foundation of the present parish of St Mildred.

The beauty of the chapel exceeded everyone's expectation. The climax of the Consecration Festival came at Evensong the next Sunday. For this the people began to fill the church a full hour before the service was due to begin and by 6.30p.m. every available inch of space was taken up. The atmosphere was electric.

The sermon, which told the story of our church, was illustrated with photographs in all its stages which vividly brought back what had been done:

Six years ago a relatively small congregation met in the little church now known as Addiscombe Hall. They were but a handful of people and they were not possessed of any material wealth. But within their sturdy souls was a gold mine: the gold mine of faith. There were many who scoffed and sneered: 'The thing can't be done'. But the congregation filled with the Spirit of God, removed the mountains of prejudice and stupidity, of selfishness and ignorance - those mighty institutions, those ancient prisons of the soul - and they conquered.

Top: *Revd Budden missed no fund-raising opportunity. The famous actress, Linda LaPlante opens the Church Bazaar in 1933, pictured here with the Revd, his wife and the owner of the Davis Theatre.*
Centre and bottom: *St Mildred's Garden Party, 1942 and Revd John Girling and Mr Hamer at the event.*
Inset: *Revd John Girling and family, 1943.*
(All pictures this page S.M.R.B.)

Other Churches

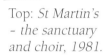

Top: *St Martin's - the sanctuary and choir, 1981.*

Above: *St Martin's memorial list of cadets from the College, 1983.*

Top right: *St Martin's from Morland Road in the summer of 1981.* (All J.P.)

Above postcard: *Mission Church, Lower Addiscombe Road near the Leslie Arms.* (B.W.)

Above: *Christ Church, Canning Road, 1905. Clyde Hall used to back on to this.* (J.G.)

Left: *St James Church, built so that cadets had somewhere to worship closer than Croydon Parish Church.* (J.G.)

⇒ Methodism ⇐

Left: Wesleyan *Methodist Church, Lower Addiscombe Road.* (J.G.)

Below: *Methodist Church, Lower Addiscombe Road, August 2000.* (S.C.)

The Wesleyan Methodist Church in Lower Addiscombe Road opened as an iron chapel in 1870. The building pictured here was consecrated on 21 September 1881, the Minister being the Revd T. Nicholson who lived at 58 Elgin Road. The church was burnt down in an arson attack on 21 January 1948.

Left: *Methodist Church, Cherry Orchard Road.* (J.G.)

Above: *Methodist Church, Cherry Orchard Road, 2000* (S.C.)

Venetian Window Blind Works,

51, LESLIE PARK ROAD, EAST CROYDON.

Private Residence: 149, Addiscombe Court Road.

R.T. WHITLOCK
(Successor to W. Slater)

Special Attention given
to Repairs of Blinds of
all kinds.

VENETIAN BLINDS
a Speciality.

Prices on Application

The Minister of Health visits Leslie Park Road Co-op Dairy in 1930. (C.L.S.L.)

Chapter 9
Shops and Businesses

by David Payne and Anne Bridge (Leslie Park Road)
and Brian Richardson (Harris & Bailey)

No.51 Leslie Park Road
(now Payne Upholstery)

Tracing the history of a building, be it a home or business premises, is a fascinating piece of detective work. Maps, deeds and directories are good sources of information, but there are many more places where one can search for clues.

Leslie Park Road was constructed some time between 1844 and 1853. It lies on what was originally 'Leslie Park' on Croydon Common and there had once been farm buildings on the site. The deeds of No.51 make fascinating reading although the legal jargon can at times be baffling. By consulting these documents together with local directories, we can piece together the story of the building.

The land occupied by No.51 formerly belonged to John Brickwood – Brickwood House stood where Brickwood Road now runs. On 19 May 1853 the land on which No.51 now stands was sold by William Berrington as part of plot 3 (out of 4) of the triangular parcel of land bounded by Leslie Park Road, Cherry Orchard Road and Lower Addiscombe Road. No.51 was sold freehold to Henry Funnell of Croydon, painter and glazier.

On 7 June 1853 Henry Funnell sold the property for £50 to Joseph Stevenson of Addiscombe, a fencing master. It can be safely assumed that Joseph Stevenson was Corporal Stevenson of the Life Guards appointed as Fencing Master to the East India Company College in 1852 shortly after the gymnasium was constructed.

On 24 October 1883 the property, including the riding stables at the back, was bought by William Slater, who already lived at 38 Leslie Park Road. William Slater ran a steam turning works on the premises and was the sole occupant until 1901. It appears that he may then have run into a spot of financial difficulty because in 1902 the front part of the property was occupied by S.C. Francis, fruiterer and greengrocer, who presumably paid him rent. In the same year on 3 June William Slater used the property as security to borrow £1800 from James Frederick William Ponsford from Shackleford, Surrey and John Scott Heron of Lawrence Lane, City of London, at a rate of interest of £5 per year.

By 1903 William Slater was being described as a blind-maker while William Burns appears to have been running the steam turning works. The property was still shared with S.C. Francis, the fruiterer and greengrocer. In 1904, however, William Slater must have retired at the age of 68. He let the premises out to William Burns, S.C. Francis and R.T. Whitlock, a blind-maker.

On 4 September 1912 William Slater died aged 75. Although still owner of the shop and former riding stables, he was living at 140 Lebanon Road. His widow, Ellen, inherited the property which on 2 October 1912 was valued at £1359. J.F.W. Ponsford and J.S. Heron, the two who had lent William Slater money against the property, had a claim to that proportion of its value that represented their loan and so they sold it jointly with Ellen Slater.

On 3 February 1912, No.51 was sold to Robert Thomas Whitlock, window blind manufacturer, who had been working on the premises since 1904. In order to do this he borrowed money from George Henry Bailey (co-founder of Harris & Bailey). No.51 stayed in the Whitlock family until on 13 March 1967 it was bought by David and Valerie Payne.

STEVENSON & SON,

RIDING, DRILLING,

AND

FENCING MASTERS,

LESLIE PARK ROAD,

CROYDON.

W. SLATER,
Steam Wood Turning Works,
51, LESLIE PARK ROAD, EAST CROYDON.

Architects' Drawings worked to.
BUILDERS' TURNERY OF ALL KINDS KEPT IN STOCK.
ALL ORDERS PUNCTUALLY ATTENDED TO.

Sid Gibbs at work in the former stables, 14 June 1974. (A.R.)

Main picture and inset: *The dismantling of the stables which had become unsafe.* (D.P.)

The shop in 2000. (S.C.)

MEMORIES OF DAVID PAYNE - LESLIE PARK ROAD

My earliest recollection of Leslie Park Road was, at the age of 11, going with my sister Pat to No.15A. My father had just started (in 1947) a business repairing furniture and upholstery - a new venture. After the Second World War new furniture was at a premium.

Our first job to help Dad was to get a bowl of water and soak off the old window stickers, advertising Phillips Sticker Soles, etc. The last tenant in the shop had been a shoe repairer - George Turner. George had moved across the road to No.51.

Dad had taken the shop on for a rental of 10 shillings (50p) a week, the going rent at the time... As time moved on I helped in the workshop as best I could. On leaving school I started as an apprentice with an established upholstery business 'Savage of Croydon'. Their workshops were in Oval Road and their main front shop was in George Street, Croydon, next to Allders Arcade.

My starting wage was £1.2s.6d. a week, of which 10 shillings went to Mum for my keep. After serving a short apprenticeship with Savage's I started with Dad. We did not have a lot of room at 15A as it was a small workshop squashed between two houses. On fine days I would work outside in the yard at the back of the workshop. As time went by I gradually picked up the skills of the trade. I remember that delivery and collection of three-piece suites from the local vicinity were upon an old hand cart - Dad pushing, and myself, with a rope around my waist, pulling from the front. Some say the good old days.

Then came National Service; after my stint in the Army it was back to work with Dad at the bench. Life in Leslie Park Road at this time was still rather peaceful. Many of the residents of the road I remember had been born there, and their parents before them. Many of them also had relations living in the road. There was one family who, come each September, would load up their old van and go off 'hopping in Kent'. No.23 was Snellings the General Grocers, on the corner of Oval Road. I remember he cooked his own hams, the smell was delicious. Across the road at No.55 was Mrs Hollamby; she sold sweets and cigarettes, plus anything else that could be crammed into the shop. Mrs Hollamby was related to the Snellings. The Co-op Bottling Plant Milk Dairy was on the corner of Lebanon Road. The Dairy started making a noise very early in the morning - the poor neighbours. They used horse-drawn milk floats and hand-pushed milk trolleys.

Another memory was Henry Streeters Haulage Lorries. These carried mostly sand and ballast and were a very scruffy fleet of lorries at the time, a bit from today - a huge company with a fleet of fine lorries. The business has long since moved from Leslie Park Road. There was another old character - Charlie Lambert - he ran the Builders Arms, a little different to the pub of today.

Payne Upholsterers are the oldest established business still remaining in the road. How time flies. Unfortunately my father died suddenly in 1960 aged 60 years. By this time we had expanded and taken over a large old barn as a workshop across the road at No.51, at the rear of the yard. The history of this old building is featured in this book, and makes very good reading.

Old George Turner was still running his shoe repair business in the front shop at No.51 - my present business premises... I can still see him, heavy canvas apron on, and covered in shoe dye and holding a heel ball. In the old building at the end of the yard, downstairs and beneath my workshop was an old builder's yard, workshop..., etc. This business was owned by Mr Whitlock. His family history went back a long way. The cottage in the yard was occupied by his elderly mother and sister (both born there).

In 1969 things were beginning to look up for me, business was expanding and I employed men to work for me. I thought I might take the plunge and managed to raise a loan to buy the whole site of No.51. I inherited four tenants, each paying me about £1.10s. a week rent. With a large bank loan this did not go far.

However, time has been good to me - hard work does pay off - and I now have a clientele stretching over a vast area - all on recommendation. I am so grateful to the loyalty of my clients of many years. Now is the time to say thank you to all of you. I am approaching my 65th birthday, but I am not yet ready to hang up my tools as I still enjoy my work so much, and meeting of many old friends and customers from past years. What more could I want?

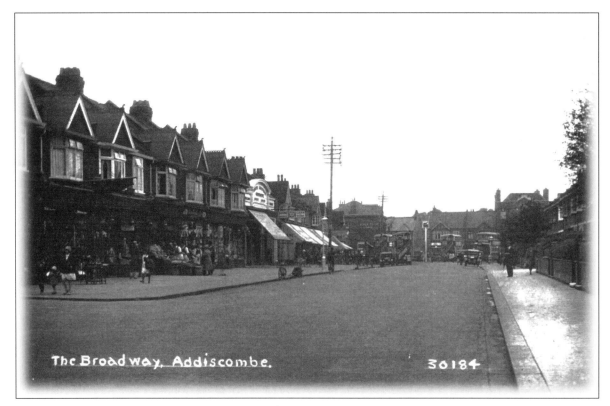

The Broadway in Lower Addiscombe, early 1930s.
The Black Horse can be seen in the distance. (B.W.)

Lower Addiscombe, early 1930s. Bingham Bridge is in the distance. (J.H.)

☞ Down Town LA! ☜

Left: *225 Lower Addiscombe Road, August 2000.* (S.C.)

Below: *Number 21 The Exchange 1915-17, now 225 Lower Addiscombe Road.* (J.G.)

Bottom: *The Exchange, Lower Addiscombe Road, 1920s. The Exchange is the stretch of shops from Inglis Road to the railway/tramline. They were built in 1907/08 on the site of a former market garden.* (J.H.)

Left: *Number 2 The Exchange is now Addiscombe DIY, formerly Mr Sealey's. It has always been a domestic stores house, the first owner being William J Phillips from 1908 to 1937. Mr Norman Green then appears to have taken over. Alec Orme owned the shop in 1951 until 1969. Here are the last three generations of owners, left to right: Mr Alec Orme (18 years), Mr Roy Sealey (26 years), Mr Bipin Panchasara (since 1995). Mr Sealey relates: 'I bought the shop from Mr Orme in 1969 after working for Nestle in Croydon for 11 years. There were four other hardware shops in Lower Addiscombe Road plus Sainsbury United Dairies but over the years, with increased rents and rates, yellow lines and competition, shops have changed hands with an increase of shops like estate agents, building societies and fast food outlets and we are now seeing the odd empty shop. In the early days we delivered paraffin and coal but with central heating and calor gas now, the sale of these items are decreasing although with decorating and gardening becoming popular you can change course. Providing goods at a fair price with service will still keep you in business.*

Above: *Bipin Panchasara serving a customer, summer 2000.*

Left: *Numbers 1-4 The Exchange, August 2000.* (Both S.C.)

HARRIS & BAILEY LIMITED

Harris & Bailey Limited are builders merchants who commenced business in 1912 as a partnership between Alfred Frank Harris and George Henry Bailey. Frank Harris had previously sold newspapers at the then busy Addiscombe Station and Bailey was a gravel merchant. Premises were rented from the London & Chatham Railway Company (later known as the Southern Railway Company) in the Addiscombe Station goods yard. Addiscombe was a 'rail head', or terminal, for that section of line and it was usual to find builders merchants in such places because at that time the majority of goods sold were delivered by railway trucks and these could then be emptied straight into the merchants' stocking area.

In 1913 a limited company was formed and Bailey departed. The entire share capital was then held by the Harris family. Judging from available records of the time, business was extremely hard and bad debts were in a similar ratio to those we see now. Trade in the early days comprised the 'heavy' side of the industry – sand, gravel, cement and bricks. As was usual in that period, coal was also sold and distributed via horse and cart to the adjoining area.

During 1935 Alfred Frank Harris died and his shareholding passed to his widow and his son, Kenneth Harris. Kenneth did not wish to be a builders merchant and had studied to be an accountant with the firm, Brown Peet & Tilly in Croydon. The principal of this firm, William Peet, by chance had a son who did not want to be an accountant. A sensible swap arrangement was agreed with Peet senr buying 50 per cent of the Harris & Bailey share capital for the benefit of his son, W. Norman Peet, who then joined straight from Whitgift School. Shortly afterwards Kenneth Harris joined Bird & Co, another firm of accountants, and was shipped off to India to work in their Calcutta office. There exists in the company's archives a correspondence file of letters from

Above: Harris & Bailey, Lower Addiscombe Road, 1950s. (C.L.S.L.) Below: Queuing for 28lb of coal at Lower Addiscombe road, 22 February, 1947. (H.B.)

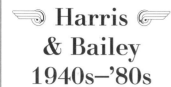

Harris & Bailey 1940s–'80s

Above: *Go get the customers, Canning Road.* (A.H.)

Above left: *Norman and Margerie Peet, and Kenneth and Mrs Harris, 1965.* (H.B.)

Left: *Harris & Bailey employees together with residents of Hastings and Warren Road celebrate the marriage of Charles and Diana.* (H.B.)

Right: *Arthur Hammond and the bad-tempered grey horse who had a tendency to bite, 1970.* (S.P.)

Left: *Queuing for coal, Lower Addiscombe Road, in the hard winter of 1946/7.* (H.B.)

Kenneth Harris to Norman Peet and vice versa from 1937 to 1951 when Kenneth finally returned from India. Norman complained bitterly about the company's performance during the pre-war and wartime period when things were at their worst for builders merchants. During the war, materials were difficult to get hold of. The company did a lot of gravel work and were on call from the Air Ministry to get hard core into Kenley and Biggin. Although the company did not make much profit during the conflict, they managed to survive. In retrospect Norman Peet had carried the load very well in this period although he received little credit for it.

Throughout the 1950s an influx of younger staff joined the company in time for the post-war boom in building. Norman Peet used to despair at the antics and short cuts employed by this younger element but was forced to admit that the results in terms of profit were encouraging. These were exciting times. It was rare to leave the office before 7.00 or 8.00p.m. and the business progressed well. Kenneth Harris returned from India to a very different environment from the one to which he had become accustomed.

The 1960s arrived and the company managed to buy the freehold of part of their rented premises. They erected a new building, completed in 1966, which pleased both staff and customers alike. Turnover and profits were still rising.

Coal continued to be delivered by horse and cart and sold locally by the sack for cash right up until the 1970s. This was known as the 'odd sack round'. The coal man had good relations with his regular customers and would give them a week's credit, even though he wasn't supposed to! The horses were stabled in Hastings Place where once Hanson Cabs had been kept for East Croydon Station.

One of the drivers, Jim Revell, used to take the horse and cart to the Easter Monday Parade in Battersea Park where he would have a good time.

Locals became used to seeing the horse and cart, apparently driverless, coming over the Windmill Bridge, its driver sleeping off the effects of the day's exertions!

During the late 1970s and early '80s, strikes became a regular feature of the industry. Supplies were often on extended delivery and it was obvious that whoever had stock could sell at almost any price. The company decided to make contact with continental suppliers. This was most unusual for a builders merchant at the time and very few contemporaries had even considered this course of action. Quick delivery of copper fittings, steel tube, and radiators led to a sharp increase in profits in this period.

In the 1980s British Rail, the landlord, eventually agreed to sell the freehold of the rest of their premises to Harris & Bailey. By now the 1966 building was outdated as the method of serving customers at the counter had changed with the influence of DIY stores. In December 1989 the current premises were completed. However, a potential disaster loomed because of the recession which hit the Western World including Great Britain. Thanks, however, to careful forward planning, following an in-depth look at similar operations in America, Europe and Scandinavia, Harris & Bailey managed to capture more than its share of available custom. This success is attributed to the simple advantage of having a customer car park capable of taking 80 vehicles, open-plan shops similar to DIY stores, while still retaining large trade counters, one for heavy materials, the other for light. At long last customers could visit a builders merchants and actually view the stock. Today sees the addition of an on-site café with full sit-down facilities, another first for builders merchants.

In the building industry it is said that, because people have to live somewhere, so there will always be a place for suppliers like Harris & Bailey!

Included in this picture are Arthur Hammond and R. Hadfield in 1970. (S.P.)

*Baldwins were situated on the corner of Cherry Orchard and Leslie Park Roads, c.1910.
There were no E.C. regulations to contend with then!* (J.G.)

*Site of former Baldwins, August 2000.
Several shops were knocked down and new ones built in 1934.* (S.C.)

F.J. Fargher, 32 Lower Addiscombe Road, c.1904 (J.G.)
and 32 Lower Addiscombe Road in August 2000. (S.C.)

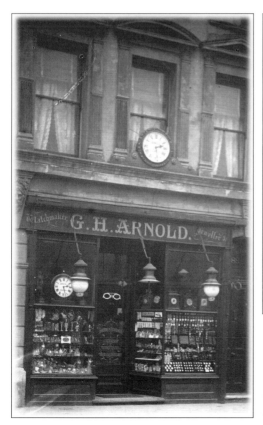

Left: *G.H. Arnold, 89 Lower Addiscombe Road.*
Prior to Mr Arnold moving in, this shop was a
confectioners and tobacconists. G.H. Arnold occu-
pied it from 1902 to 1919. He had an assistant, D.H.
Dore, who became sole occupant from 1920. (J.G.)
Above: *89 Lower Addiscombe Road today.* (S.C.)

166. CHERRY ORCHARD ROAD CROYDON. 1909

FRED. THORNTON,
Slater and Tiler,
129, ✦ CHERRY ✦ ORCHARD ✦ ROAD,
EAST CROYDON.

DRAINS attended to, Chimney Pots Re-fixed, and Contracts entered into for the Repair of Slate and Tile Roofs. Slating and Tiling at per square.

ESTIMATES GIVEN.

Special attention is given to the Repairing of Roofs.

All Orders promptly attended to.

Left: Goddards, 166 Cherry Orchard Road, Christmas 1909. (J.G.)

Below left: Cherry Orchard Road. (J.G.)

Below right: 101 Lower Addiscombe Road has always sold wines and spirits and initially was also a grocers! Former occupants have been H. Grimbleby (1876-97), Collis Clark (1898-1902), Arthur Peerless (1903-10), Harry Cusden (1911) and Harry Leppard from 1912 until well into the 1960s. Modern-day picture, August 2000. (S.C.)

Bottom: *Lower Addiscombe Road on the corner of Cherry Orchard Road, c.1910.* (J.G.)

ADDISCOMBE.
Collis Clark's Stores.
Tea, Coffee, Grocery,
Provisions, Wines, Spirits,
Bottled Beers, &c. &c.

BEST QUALITY ONLY
AT
LOWEST CASH PRICES.

COMPARISON INVITED.

101, Lr. Addiscombe Road.
Telephone No. 74. Croydon.

LOWER ADDISCOMBE ROAD. 3   A.W.S. SERIES.

Lower Addiscombe Road and corner of Warren Road between 1902 and 1927. (C.L.S.L.)

Lower Addiscombe Road and corner of Warren Road, August 2000. (S.C.)

Left: *John Kirkby White Metalworker, August 2000.* (S.C.)

Below left: *Jim from Prawnbrokers 203, Lower Addiscombe Road, August 2000. Below is one of his favourite recipes.*

Above: *Arthur's the Barbers, Lower Addiscombe Road, August 2000.*
(All photographs this page S.C.)

STEAMED SEA BASS WITH GINGER AND SPRING ONIONS
(Salmon or Halibut steaks can also be used)

INGREDIENTS
1-1$^{1}/_{2}$ lb sea bass, scaled, trimmed, gutted and scored ('Jim the Fish' will do this for you)
$^{1}/_{2}$ teaspoon salt
1 tablespoon sesame oil
2-3 spring onions cut in half lengthways
2 tablespoons light Soy sauce
2 tablespoons rice wine or dry sherry
1 tablespoon finely shredded ginger

FOR GARNISH
2 tablespoons shredded spring onion
2 tablespoons finely shredded carrot

METHOD
Rub the sea bass inside and out with the salt and sesame oil.
Sprinkle the spring onions over a heat-proof platter and place the fish on top.
Blend together the rice wine, Soy sauce and the shredded ginger and pour evenly over the fish.
Place the platter in a very hot steamer (or inside a wok on a rack) and steam vigorously covered for 12-15 minutes.
Heat the sesame oil until hot.
Remove the platter from the steamer, place the shredded spring onion and carrot on top of the fish and pour the oil over the fish.
Serve immediately.

Chapter 10
Trains, Trams, Boats & Planes

by Steve Collins, David Delaney, Steve Earl, Anne Bridge and Peter Little

With the explosive growth of our and other local suburbs, came an increasing demand for better transport, to convey both goods and the increasing populace. One cannot build houses (villas) without heavy materials, and the incoming occupants needed to travel to work to pay the rent. They also needed fuel and food. Here follows an almost Darwinian history of our local transport systems which sees one system evolving out of another. In the case of trams, we seem to have created a 'round robin'!

At the time of development, the motivators in transportation systems were private, subscription-based companies - perhaps the DOT.COMS of the day. All of what we describe were major engineering projects, fabulously expensive, and in need of hefty investment. They drew upon the technologies of the day, raised monies and got on with the job in hand. All of this involved local labour, but when imported, labourers typically stayed.

You may be surprised to note Addiscombe's connection with boats and planes so let us start with the boats. Apart from horse carts, the only type of early bulk transport system was the Croydon Canal. David Delaney reports...

CROYDON CANAL

If one looks north from the line of the Lower Addiscombe Road, one can see the prominent ridge now known as Crystal Palace which is crowned by two transmitter masts. As one begins to walk in that direction one becomes aware that one is walking on a gentle down gradient, and it is this slight slope that ensures that the Norbury Brook (also known as the River Graveney) eventually flows into the River Wandle. The source of the Norbury Brook now lies hidden under modern roads and building and its course only becomes definite below the playground of the Davidson Road School, from where it crosses the extensive railway working of Selhurst and then emerges on the surface for the first time in Hever Meadow.

At this point the land has sloped from Lower Addiscombe's 51 metres above sea level to Hever Meadow's 47.5 metres and it is convenient to think of this latter contour line as the northern boundary of the Addiscombe area, provided that is that we always remember that the modern ground levels do not exactly correspond to the natural levels that existed before modern development occurred. It is important to make this point because 200 years ago, the contour line from what is now West Croydon Station all the way to what is now Forest Hill Station had been chosen as the route of a new canal - the Croydon Canal which eventually reached the Thames at Rotherhithe. For our purposes we shall restrict ourselves to the short section that we can think of as Addiscombe's northern boundary and this is now covered by the line of the West Croydon to New Cross Gate railway. Two centuries ago the railway did not exist. In fact, the land was a very unexploited mix of common land and farmed land and the cutting of a canal through the heavy clay from Croydon across the Croydon Common and on towards the Jolly Sailor's pub was the first stage in the sequence of changes that take us from open country to the present dense development.

The background is that, 200 years ago land transport had become a major problem. Everything depended upon the muscle power of men and horses. The roads were generally in poor, unsurfaced condition and experiments were being made in the use of tramways (horse-drawn, of course) and in the construction of waterways, again where horses would provide the motive power.

Right: *General route of Croydon Canal showing locks and bridges.*

Top left: Former path of Croydon canal.

Left: Woodside Station, 1950. (L.B.H.)

Above: Spurgeon's Bridge - the present West Croydon line was built on the bed of the canal. (D.D.)

Above: Addiscombe Station Entrance Hall mid 1950s. (L.B.H.)

Right: Addiscombe Station mid 1940s showing extended platforms and canopies. Lever signal box in distance at end of platform (L.B.H.)

In the 1790s a grand scheme was afoot to link the major naval establishments at Chatham and Portsmouth with a canal which would pass through, or at least close to, Croydon. In the event, the scheme, proposed by the famous engineer John Rennie, was too ambitious and too expensive to be pursued, but canals were built from the Thames at Rotherhithe to Croydon and this was a major factor in Croydon's remarkable growth throughout the 19th century and beyond. The Croydon Canal was officially opened in September 1809. It was 34 feet wide at the surface, had a central channel that was 5 or 6 feet deep, and was built to take barges of up to 50 feet in length by up to 9 feet in width. The maximum carrying capacity of a barge was about 35 tonnes. An auctioneer's notice survives referring to the sale of one of these Capital Class barges and a pencilled note at the bottom records that the barge was sold for £94.

Although there are no obvious signs that the Croydon Canal passed the Addiscombe area, one can still walk along the canal route because in 1836 the Company of the proprietors of the Croydon Canal sold out to the London and Croydon Railway Company who used the canal land as the basis for the West Croydon to New Cross Gate railway route. Stand at West Croydon Station and one is standing where the canal's terminal basin once existed, and from there to Selhurst the railway exactly follows the line once used by the canal. The railway runs over the infilled bed of the canal. From Selhurst to Norwood Junction Station railway and canal took slightly different curved lines, but again with the result that the canal has been obliterated. From the platforms at West Croydon one can see the canal/railway line taking a steady right curve to reach the first landmark which is Spurgeon's Bridge. This name was adopted after the building of West Croydon Baptist Church which was popularly known as 'Spurgeon's Tabernacle' after the great preacher John Haddon Spurgeon.

Prior to the building of this church the bridge carrying St James's Road over the Croydon Canal had been known as Brick Bridge. The south side of the bridge is still a brick structure and looks remarkably like a canal bridge though it is most likely a railway-era structure. The canal, like the present railway, passes through a 30-foot deep cutting, the deepest cutting on the canal's route.

From Spurgeon's Bridge there is a footpath running alongside the railway and this path is very close to the original line of the canal towpath. This footpath, officially referred to as Footpath No.672, reaches Sydenham Road after 450 yards and it is worth saying that the road bridge, sometimes said to be a canal-era bridge is almost certainly a product of the railway engineers. Just look at the size of the massive girders supporting the road – it is certainly not pre-1840s.

West Croydon line on the bed of the canal.
(D.D.)

On the north side of the bridge we find the Bird in Hand pub, recently re-named the Bird of Pride, and this has been said to be an inn dating from canal days. Not so. The first record of a building on this site dates from 1831 (at which time the canal still had 5 years of life left) but it is not until 1874 (some 36 years after the closure of the canal) that we find a reference to it being used as a beer-house. Footpath No.672 continues across the road for another 290 yards to reach the Gloucester Road bridge, another railway-era structure. Of particular note is the low wall on the south east corner, for this retaining wall is in the right place to have been part of the tow-path structure and whilst it has been repaired in places, the original brickwork looks as though it possibly could date from canal days. Perhaps this is Croydon's only above ground canal remnant – so little but that's part of its charm. Incidentally, Footpath No.672 always used to be known locally as the Cinder Bank or the Cinder Path, though no-one seems to know the origin of the name or where the cinders came from. It is likely that the canal towpath ran parallel and at a lower level, quite close to the present rail ballast which itself is probably on the same level as the surface of the old canal. Beyond Gloucester Road the footpath has been blocked off where it continues behind the Roman Industrial Estate.

So far it is easy to look at the railway and imagine it as it looked from 1809–36, a busy waterway with

loaded boats each with a crew of two men and a boy to look after the horse. The men earned 3s.6d. each per day, and the boy and horse earned 2s.3d. From Gloucester Road to Norwood Junction it is difficult to gain any idea of how the scene looked so long ago, for railway requirements have totally re-shaped the land and changed original levels. But the canal did pass this way in a great curve around Addiscombe's northern boundary and crossed Tennison Road on its way to pass close to the Jolly Sailor's pub. When the canal was built, Croydon was a busy, compact town of under 6000 inhabitants. The 1801 census had recorded 5743 people in this the largest town south of London. Less than 50 years later the 1847 census showed 13 627 inhabitants and the Croydon Canal had played a part in bringing about this growth. It had enabled the transportation of timber and bricks to speed development, and had broadened the range of heavy and bulky goods that could be moved economically, but its main contribution lay in the events of 1836 when it was decided to sacrifice it to the cause of rail transport. Having cost in the region of £160 000 to build, the canal was sold to the Proprietors of the proposed London and Croydon Railway for a bargain £40 250. Parliament had ruled that there should be only one railway south of London, and by cutting the Croydon Canal into unusable fragments the railway simultaneously gained a reasonable though not ideal route and eliminated a possible competitor. Addiscombe came so close to inheriting a waterway of enormous amenity value right on its northern boundary but the only obvious indications now are the aptly named Canal Way and Towpath Walk where once the waterway ran. And as you can see, water transport fell out of fashion, the canal beds were drained, which provided a golden opportunity for the railway companies to move in.

Given that canals were generally designed to avoid any undue gradient (lock), had a secure ground bed and were of a sufficient width for a railway, it was decided to lay track and install telegraph and communications systems.

Gloucester Road Bridge. (D.D.)

ATMOSPHERIC RAILWAYS

(With acknowledgement to Charles Hadfield for his book Atmospheric Railways *(Newton Abbot, 1967).*

In 1845 Lord Bacon giving evidence to the Parliamentary Gauge Inquiry that would standardise how far apart rail lines should be (there was great debate as to whether it should be narrow or broad – the Brunel following favouring the latter). He said:

There be three things that make a nation great and prosperous – a fertile soil, busy workshops and easy conveyance for men and commodities from one place to another.

How true this is. Let us begin with the Croydon Atmospheric Railway. This was, amongst others, a Brunel inspired idea that basically involved dragging a train down the track by vacuum power. Within the track bed there was a pipe, in which a piston that was attached to the train connected.

The Atmospheric Railway provided a real alternative to the steam engine. It was cheaper, faster, was virtually silent and, astonishingly, could cope with steeper gradients than the steam engines.

All of this involved huge pumping stations along the line to evacuate the driving tube that was gasket sealed with leather. Four such railways were built and operated at times between 1844 and 1860. (More about pumping stations later – see the neat move that Latham made to turn air (or lack of it) into water for the area!).

Early in August 1844 the London & Croydon Railway was authorised to build a third track for atmospheric trains on the east side of its existing lines from Corbett's Lane (the junction with the London & Greenwich), to Jolly Sailor (the junction for the Brighton line) – and from there to Croydon. One of the two existing lines would be converted to atmospheric. With the planned extension to Epsom (see Entertainment: Ashburton Racecourse for the Epsom link), it was reckoned that they would have to lay about 20 miles of tube.

After much argy-bargy over cross charging between different rail operators (not much has changed), the company's senior engineer, Cubitt, appointed Charles H. Gregory as assistant engineer for the atmospheric lines. They started with the five-mile section from Croydon to Dartmouth Arms (on 3 July 1845 the name was changed to Forest Hill and Jolly Sailor was also changed to Norwood – see Croydon Pubs section).

In January 1845 Cubitt approved the design for the timber viaduct that was to carry the atmospheric track at a 1-in-50 gradient over the Brighton & Dover lines at Norwood, and so construction started.

Then the problems began. By February 1845 none of the 15" tubes (for the vacuum) had arrived! When they did, the proportion of breakages was high. These were sourced from the Coalbrookdale Company but Coalbrookdale had been casting cylinders since the 1720s under the leadership of Abraham Darby, and carefully open sand cast the whole structure for the first iron bridge over the Severn. The tubes had been shipped by tramroad to the head of the Shropshire Canal, then by tug-boats to the Birmingham & Liverpool Junction Canal, before being put on to 20-tonne narrowboats to Brentford for further transhipment by barges to our area.

All of this resulted in considerable spat. Coalbrookdale blamed the Company's unloading and design, and the Company blamed them for flaws in their manufacturing process.

In mid March 1845, rails and sleepers were on the ground, but by June – even though the stationary engine houses at Croydon, Norwood and Forest Hill were ready – the evacuating pumps had not been delivered. With regard to the Croydon and Epsom line, it was determined by the architects that the pumping stations '... should have character, and to relieve their baldness by the addition of proportions and decorations that have hitherto belonged to the bell-towers of early Gothic churches'. The stationary engines were delivered late, arriving in July 1845; they were quickly installed and proven. By 21 August 1845 the tubes were in place, cleaned down, and on the following day, the first tests were held using a Norwood engine only. Everyone was happy – the test atmospheric train overtook the Brighton train of

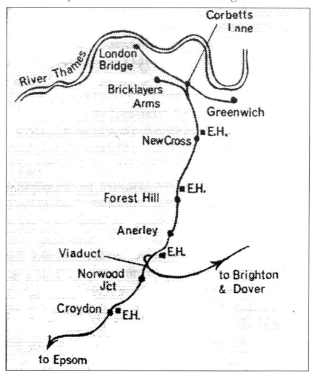

The London & Croydon Railway, planned route 1844.

seven carriages, pulled by two steam loco's (the track was aligned in places) at an astonishing 60mph. In September 1845, the atmospheric train reached 70mph with six carriages and 30mph sucking sixteen carriages. Just imagine the effort that was needed - ingenuity, project management, commercial dealings - all vital to achieve this result so quickly !

However, there were many problems, the most important of which was gasket sealing with the under track tube. But a regular timetable was operated, and in the five months from February until June 1846 a monthly average of 81 642 passengers used the service - a 24 per cent increase over the previous year.

This is an interesting statistic, since the new Tramlink scheme claims to carry around 300 000 passengers per month (Roger Harding, Tramlink, September 2000), after some six months of operational service. It is estimated that some two out of three passengers have free or pre-paid (through other operators) tickets. In the year 2000 there are around 330 000 people living in Croydon. In 1851 there were 20 548, so pro-rata, it seems as though the Atmospheric Railway was on to a good thing.

And now for the demise ... The 10 October 1846 edition of the usually moderate *Railway Chronicle* ran a damning report after canvassing the opinions of daily City Commuters. The essence was '... irregularity, slowness, continual uncertainty and disappointment'.

For the line's first six months, the engines had been blamed, then the sealing valve, and then lack of water to drive the huge evacuating steam pumps. There were also problems because they could only go forwards (along with the 'suck'), could not reverse and often overshot the makeshift station platforms.

Operating expenses were also much greater than expected. But the Epsom extension was almost ready to meet the demands of the 15 May 1847 race

Atmospheric Railway train on Croydon Line with driver c1845. The driver is screwing down the brake. Behind him the gauge shows the vacuum. The lever in front probably works a valve in the piston acting as an emergency brake. (P.T.)

traffic. So what to do? The Board decided that there should be no further investment in atmospheric transport, and that (steam) locomotives would be used instead.

Within a few weeks orders were given to dismantle the wooden viaducts, let the engine houses, sell the engines and tubes, and to withdraw the Bill enforcing the additional line to London Bridge.

At the end of May 1847, shareholders were told that by the advice of their Consulting Engineer, and with the sanction of the Railway Commissioners, 'we have substituted Locomotive power'. So this was the end of the line for Croydon's Atmospheric Railway. Steam trains became the norm instead. It was terminal.

ADDISCOMBE & WOODSIDE AND OTHER LOCAL STATIONS *by Steve Earl & Steve Collins*

So here we are with steam-train traction. What happened next to address the obvious passenger patronage? As early as 6 June 1863 an advertisement in the *Croydon Chronicle* announced the sale of building land on the former East India Company Estate. Part of the attraction was the new Addiscombe Station 'bringing the property in constant communication with the City and West End at all times of the day'. The Addiscombe branch line is part of the South Eastern Railways (SER) 'Mid-Kent' line. It ran from Lewisham, via Lower Sydenham, to what is now Beckenham Junction and came into use on 1 January 1857.

The SER line was extended with a three-and-a-quarter-mile extension to Croydon (Addiscombe Road as it was then known, now the Lower Addiscombe Road) on 1 April 1864. This broke the monopoly of Croydon traffic that had previously been enjoyed by the London, Brighton & South Coast Railway (LB&SCR).

The original 1864 Addiscombe station, like the original at Hayes, was a modest 'clapboard' structure with a simple canopy part way down on the 'up' platform, a turntable at the platform end adjoining Lower Addiscombe Road (now under the site of the present 1899 Station Building), and a small engine shed.

There were no goods traffic facilities at the time, but these were soon to follow. The idea was to serve the transport needs of the occupants of the increasing number of Addiscombe villas – some of which, were being developed by, believe it or not, a Mr Addiscombe Thorne!

As early as 1869 Addiscombe Station enjoyed a service of 19 trains per weekday and 4 trains on

Atmospheric Railway Engine House in its original position at West Croydon later to become the Surrey Street Pumping Station. See Latham (Local Heroes) to discover how this was moved. (I.L.N.)

Addiscombe Station, 1899. (C.L.S.L.)

Woodside Station, c.1910. (J.H.)

Sunday. The rapid growth in the suburban traffic resulted in the opening of Woodside Station in 1871. The station served the district of South Norwood and the nearby Croydon Racecourse. Woodside's major traffic were the racecourse specials. Horses were transported by train and for a number of years a track to the course from the 'Down' side of the station catered for many famous horses of the time. A doorway with a high arch existed close to the ticket barrier, constructed so that horses could reach the adjacent Ashburton Park without climbing to road level.

The biggest event was the annual March United Kingdom Grand Handicap steeplechase - equivalent to that of Epsom in flat racing. In 1887, the year of Queen Victoria's Golden Jubilee, some 10 500 schoolchildren joined in celebrations on the racecourse after journeying there via Woodside Station. This was at the height of the racecourse's popularity.

The SER opened a branch line to Hayes on 29 May 1882 and followed up with a joint SER/LBSCR line between Woodside and Selsdon on 10 August 1885. This linked both the Mid-Kent line with the South Croydon-East Grinstead line which had opened on the 10 March 1884.

By 1885 Addiscombe Station was enjoying 25 trains each way per weekday and 4 of a Sunday, with a direct service to Liverpool Street (the terminus of the Great Eastern Railway) via the newly constructed spurs on to the East London Line near New Cross Station, and then through the Thames Tunnel.

During this period the Hayes branch which had opened on 29 May 1882 was celebrating three years of service. To cope with the additional traffic, Elmers End Station had been completely rebuilt and provided with additional facilities - including the existing platform height raised and two new bays provided. The 'up' side was designated for the use of Addiscombe, and the 'down' side bay for the Hayes branch traffic. A new station building was erected, a footbridge built to connect the platforms, and a superb Saxby & Farmer 43-lever frame signal box installed to control traffic between the two diverging lines.

By 1897 the area around the Addiscombe branch had become much more built-up with residential developments on both sides of the line - Warren, Hastings Roads (occupying a site of a former brickworks) to the West, and to the East, Grant Road.

In the 1890s the SER realised that the original station at Addiscombe could not cope with the increased local usage and plans were drawn up to replace it with a larger and more permanent structure. Work was carried out between 1896-99. Tired of ruinous competition the SER and LC&DR amalgamated, and so the South Eastern & Chatham Railway (SECR) came into being on 1 January 1899 - but did not receive Royal Assent until 5 August 1899.

The new Addiscombe Station was much larger than its predecessor. It comprised a main red-brick building (still existent today) that had a gated forecourt. This was built on the site of the original turntable. As it was felt that turning facilities were still necessary, a replacement turntable was installed at the opposite end of the station, just to the west of the running lines.

The main building contained the booking hall, parcels and left luggage offices and a number of waiting rooms - especially for first-class ticket holders.

The signalling arrangements had to be extensively revised to cater for the new layout and a new 47-lever box replaced the original 1864 model.

Addiscombe Station could now meet the increased demand, but still could not compete with the nearby LB&SCR Station at East Croydon. As an example, in 1910 the stopping train into Cannon Street from Addiscombe took 40 minutes, whilst the East Croydon service to the City was quicker. With a regular electric tram service from Addiscombe to East Croydon (1902) this made the journey complete.

To counter, just prior to the first world war, the Addiscombe 'Flyer' service was introduced - departing from Addiscombe at 7:20a.m., calling at Woodside, then non-stop to London Bridge and Cannon Street where it terminated at 7:46a.m.

Just think about this. A journey time to the City of 26 minutes with steam traction takes some beating. The 'Flyer' was of obvious appeal to the Addiscombe professional populace (see Villas Galore). The journey time from East Croydon station to the City is currently (year 2000) around 20 minutes, and the travel time to East Croydon from Addiscombe by the new Tramlink service will add a further 10 minutes to the journey - so not much has changed!

Having settled the problems of passenger overcrowding, SECR then turned their attention to freight facilities. In the period 1903-10, long and bay sidings were introduced for storage of empty carriage stock and heavy freight.

In 1911 the line saw an increase to 34 trains per weekday and 13 each Sunday, and the Great Northern opened its own coal siding (see Harris & Bailey).

Further improvement to the rail service and facilities took a back seat with the advent of the First World War. Forced onto an austerity war footing, SECR had to dispense with any 'unnecessary items' for the duration of the conflict. They de-manned and closed stations and halts. The first was Bingham Road, and then the Spencer Road Halt in March 1915 - which was never to re-open again. The Coombe Road station was closed in January 1917.

During the war SECR found accommodation for Belgian railwaymen who had fled their country

Addiscombe Station

Left: *Addiscombe Station in 1905.*

Right: *Addiscombe Station in 1919.* (Both J.G.)

Left: *Addiscombe station, c.1920.* (J.G.)

Below: *Addiscombe Station J Class Steam Train.* (S.E.)

Bottom left: *Addiscombe 47 Lever Signal Box.* (P.O.)

because of invasion. In October 1914, Belgian State Railway officers and their families were boarded in the Charing Cross and Cannon Street Station Hotels at SECR expense. In January 1915 Belgian refugees were being employed as platelayers (laying railway lines) over the entire SECR network - including the Addiscombe branch. In 1920 the sidings were extended for goods traffic for Harris & Bailey.

The Railways Act of 1921 saw the grouping of companies into four large concerns, and locally the SECR - along with the LBSCR and LSWR - was to become part of the Southern Railway Company as of 1 January 1923.

The Southern improved services on all lines - including the Addiscombe Branch - and by 1924 there were 38 trains per weekday and 15 each Sunday - all steam hauled.

Southern Railway had to move with the times and move to electrification - particularly to beat the growing threat of improved tram services. The Southern had inherited a rag-bag of electrical traction systems, some overhead, some 'third' rail. Finally they went for the third rail system and the Addiscombe line (and its neighbours) got turned on!

Addiscombe Road Station had its name changed in 1925. It had been known as Croydon (Addiscombe Road) between 1864 and 1925, then briefly as Croydon (Addiscombe), and in March 1926 it simply became Addiscombe Station.

In 1925 the Southern was approached by the Metropolitan Railway with grand plans for extending the East London line trains beyond New Cross and terminating them at Addiscombe - it had the room. By the end of 1925 the 'Met' had gone as far as drawing up a timetable for through trains between Hammersmith and Addiscombe with a start date of January 1926. The first train would leave Hammersmith at 8:01a.m. and arrive at 9:12a.m. And from Addiscombe to Hammersmith there would be a 7:53a.m. train with the last train at 21:35p.m.

In modern times, anyone who lives in the Addiscombe area and needs to travel to West London - let us say that you work for the BBC - will know what a horrendous journey it currently is by public transport. The idea of a journey time of an hour and a quarter would be ideal today and unheard of during the 1920s.

The Metropolitan proposal was sound, but foundered because of disparate (Southern/Met) electrical provision and the high voltage danger to the Met's motor cars (engines). There also was an emerging danger about loading gauges. In any event, a trial was run on 17 February 1926 between New Cross and Addiscombe using steam traction. This was the make or break test and was judged not to be successful.

The idea of the Hammersmith-Addiscombe service was mooted again in 1929 and finally abandoned in 1930. Pity really!

During this period Addiscombe Station had seen some changes. A huge EMU (Electrical Mechanical Unit - electric train to you and me) shed was constructed in 1925. The first-class waiting room was converted into an enginemen's and motormen's lobby and the southern went electric! Elmers End to Hayes was electrified on 21 September 1925 and Addiscombe was fully electrically powered by 28 February 1926.

All trains to Addiscombe were distinguished by their 'T' headcode. In July 1926 there was a train every half-hour with a semi-fast journey time of under 25 minutes. The electrification and expansion policy paid off. In 1936, Addiscombe had 59 trains per weekday and each Sunday.

Left: *1924 type 4 SUBS ready to leave London Bridge in rush hour. The 'T' headcode for Addiscombe; the other train for Dartford.* (I.A.)

Aerial view of Addiscombe Station, July 1992, with Harris & Bailey centre right and the EMU sheds to the left. (S.E.)

THE RAILWAYS IN WARTIME

The coming of war in September 1939 saw drastic reductions under the war economy measures. Emergency cuts in passenger services introduced on 16 October 1939 resulted in Addiscombe being served by a shuttle to and from Elmers End only. This was known as the 'Popper'.

As with other members of the 'Big Four' railway companies, the Southern had to cope with increased traffic – especially military, evacuation and the general transport of vital materials and goods. As a consequence, the Luftwaffe bombed the rail network. Hayes Station had its entrance badly damaged on 15 September 1940. Astonishingly, repairs were not completed until BR times in 1956. The 'down' side of Hayes Station was badly damaged in early 1941, and an Addiscombe train (in a bay) received a direct hit a few months later. Addiscombe Station survived the bombing, but lost all of its ornate original SER wrought iron work from the roof, the forecourt railings, its gates and even the lamps – all to do with the scrap drive to assist the war effort.

After the war, a degree of normality slowly returned, but one which was hampered by the prevailing austerity of the time. A Labour government was voted in, and the railways were nationalised in 1948 under the Railways Act of 1947. The spring of 1948 saw the return of trains between Addiscombe and central London, with the shuttle for Sunday services.

Attempts to improve the declining services on the Southern Region included the use of 'double-decker' stock, but suffered from height clearance difficulties and the time it took passengers to get on and off. BR decided on lengthening all station platforms to accommodate 10-car sets. In March 1956, the 'Island Platform' (one and two) were extended to the signal box. The eight-car capacity platform three was demolished and the site used as an additional stabling siding.

Despite these changes, in September 1958 Addiscombe Station had its service cut from four trains an hour to a half-hourly service – all as a consequence of increased road traffic competition. Road traffic competition also spelt the decline and closure of the Goods Yards on the lines. The Woodside Station Yard closed on 30 September 1963, the Hayes Station Yard with its seven-tonne capacity crane in April 1965 and the Addiscombe Yards on 17 June 1968.

The Woodside Signal box lost its importance when the Woodside to Selsdon line was closed on 13 May 1983 and was finally shut down on 24 June 1984. In fact, Woodside Station became the first unstaffed station on the line in 1993. And then the Tramlink scheme came along. The 1993 Tramlink Bill required use of the Woodside, Bingham Road and Coombe Road track beds to enable the new Tram system.

An earlier Tramlink route proposal involved Addiscombe Station. This would have used the existing station site with tram lines feeding and returning using the almost directly opposite Canning and Clyde roads to gain access to the Chepstow/Addiscombe Road interchange. With fierce local opposition, this route plan was fortunately abandoned. The writing was on the wall for the local stations. The huge EMU shed at Addiscombe was closed in 1993. On the evening of 7 March 1996 the superb Addiscombe signal box was deliberately burnt down.

Right:
Addiscombe Station, July 2000. (A.B.)

The well known Alice - a great signal woman at Addiscombe box c.1994. (P.O.)

Addiscombe Station entrance hall, mid 1950s. (B.H.)

Addiscombe Station ran its last train on Saturday 31 May 1997 with a commemorative 'Networker' Unit No:466016 shuttling back and forth to Elmers End. Since that time, Addiscombe Station has been left to deteriorate. All of the platform canopies have been removed - and more. The property owners - Railtrack - wish to develop the site for housing. Huge attendance at local meetings reveal that this is not a popular option. The South East and Chatham Railway (SECR) Preservation Society wish to use the site as a working railway museum, and have planning permission to do so. We understand that a Croydon Council decision will be taken before the end of the year 2000 to decide the fate of this excellent 1864 piece of transportation.

Before departing from Addiscombe Station - let us leave with a spooky story concerning the huge EMU shed. A number of signalmen reported hearing the distinctive rumble of a train leaving the shed at night. And, when they went to check what was going on, they found that all was still and every handbrake firmly wound down. Other phenomena have included a grey figure leaving the sheds and walking along the track. This has been seen by drivers and a particular shunter who - on

turning to get a better look at the figure's blurred features - found that the strange form had disappeared!

Although the shed had four roads (tracks), it was very unusual for any train to be berthed in road four. Shunters and cleaners reported that this road was much colder than the rest - for no obvious reason. It transpires, however, that a shunter was crushed and killed while coupling a train on road four. Other staff were killed in the shed by a water boiler exploding. On another occasion, a driver, second man and blacksmith were killed when a train ran through the end of the shed, crashing into the smithy situated behind the building.

The identity of the ghost(s) remains a mystery, but many think that the main paranormal force is the ghost of the shunter from No. four road.

Right: *EMU Sheds.* (B.H.)

Below: *EMU sheds, 1999.* (P.O.)

Addiscombe extended platforms with original signal box, late 1960s. (P.O.)

Addiscombe Station from signal box. (P.O.)

⟨ Bingham ⟩ Bridge

Left: *Bingham Bridge was a famous landmark on the Woodside to Selsdon Railway. Trams terminated here at Bingham Halt. This picture shows Bingham Bridge before 1907.* (R.W.)

Right: *The low Bingham railway bridge did not restrict the use of double-decker buses on the Lower Addiscombe Road but other tall vehicles came unstuck (or stuck).* (J.K.)

Below: *Bingham Halt, beneath the bridge, c.1930.* (C.L.S.L.)

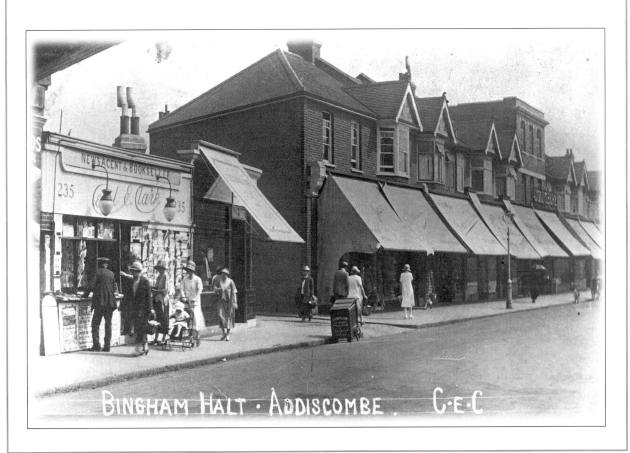

BINGHAM HALT · ADDISCOMBE. C·E·C

This page: *The Bingham Bridge was finally demolished on 13 May 1990 to make way for the new Tramlink scheme. The tram design aim was to always work at ground level , so this meant removing the bridge and the surrounding embankments. The major earth works involved – and the result of them – caused serious flooding to the Addiscombe shopping centre. The Tramlink consortium were therefore forced to introduce major new drains which further served to delay the opening of the Tram system.* (Picture S.H.)

Right: *The last day of tram operation, Leslie Arms, 31 March 1927.* (C.L.S.L.)

Below: *Tram Lower Addiscombe Road by Bingham Bridge, some time between 1902 and 1906.* (J.G.)

TRAMS IN ADDISCOMBE: THE FIRST ERA
by Anne Bridge

The Government authorised the first horse-drawn tramway in Croydon in 1878. By 1880 there existed two separate lines operating along Brighton Road and south of High Street. In 1883 Alderman A.T. Layton living in Woodside decided it was about time that a tram came their way. A boom ensued. The history of the first tramways in Croydon is one of constant changes in ownership and of constant adaptation to ever-evolving circumstances.

The Norwood District Tramway had been formed in 1882. It merged with the Croydon Tramways Company on 2 August 1883 to form the Croydon & Norwood Tramways Company. Very soon afterwards, the system was leased to the Steam Tramways Traction Company who became the operating company (but not the owners). Despite their name, they used the hairy kind of horse power.

By 1883 Route 3 was running from East Croydon Station to Leslie Arms in Cherry Orchard Road, past Addiscombe Road Station and Woodside Racecourse to Portland Road Station terminating at the Signal Hotel in South Norwood. To serve this route a depot was built by Woodside Station. The horse-drawn trams were single decker so they could pass under the Bingham Bridge and on to Woodside Racecourse. The closure of the racecourse in 1890 led to a drop in passenger numbers as the stretch after Addiscombe Road Station along the Lower Addiscombe Road had hardly been built up. So for a while the Addiscombe tram line only operated between George Street and the Alma Tavern. A service was also maintained between the Woodside Depot and the Signal Hotel.

The Croydon & Norwood Tramways Company assumed operation of the trams on 1 January 1885. In May 1888 they went into liquidation and a new company, reviving the name Croydon Tramways Company, was formed to take over the system from the liquidator on 1 January 1889.

Croydon tram horses were reputedly fine animals and figured splendidly at the Annual Horse Show. A bell was tied to the horses' collars to warn pedestrians of the tram's approach. This was particularly important at night as the trams were lit only by a dim paraffin lamp at each end. During the 1880s a flat fare of 2d. for any distance on each route was charged but passengers changing route had to pay again. The horse-drawn trams moved at a leisurely pace. The drivers and conductors worked the same route year after year. The driver stood all day on the front platform braving the elements. He wore a large leather apron and in bad weather a shiny black tarpaulin and sou'wester. Passengers often stood on the front platform providing (usually) welcome company to the driver.

Tram by Addiscombe Railway Station. (J.G.)

Tram by Alma Tavern. (J.G.)

By the end of the 19th century the track and cars were in a sorry state and Croydon Corporation acquired the system. On 1 January 1900 the British Electric Traction Company took over the working of the existing system and it was reconstructed and electrified by the British Thomson Houston Company. The last horse-drawn tram on the Addiscombe Line ran to Bingham Road on 3 January 1902.

ELECTRIC POWER

The new, heavier electric powered trams required new track and elegantly wrought standards to carry the electric cable. The British Thomson–Houston Company Limited undertook the work quickly and efficiently. On the Addiscombe Line, track was laid from a spur from the main line at Crown Hill to George Street, past East Croydon Station, along Cherry Orchard Road, turning right at the Leslie Arms into Lower Addiscombe Road, past the Addiscombe Road Railway Station and Alma Tavern and, as with the original horse-drawn tram line, on to Bingham Road Bridge. This terminus had the advantage of creating a significant interchange for passengers from Woodside Station arriving at Bingham Halt Railway Station.

The route was single track throughout with 13 passing loops over its length. On the bend between Outram and Havelock Roads were light signals triggered automatically by the trams.

Above and left: Passing loops between Outram and Havelock Roads, 1913 (J.G.) *and the same view in August 2000.* (S.C.)

Croydon Corporation Tramway Band. (J.H.)

The first new electric Addiscombe tram ran on 4 January 1902. The new red trams created quite a stir. In 1901 'Argus' in the *Croydon Advertiser* had remarked on electric trams on one of the other lines:

No, it can't be Croydon. To see those huge cars going along, driven and lit by electricity, as light as day inside at night, and travelling over ground safely, luxuriously, rapidly, was a sight which an old inhabitant must have marvelled at, and even the new inhabitant must have wondered about.

Moreover, the four Croydon lines carried different coloured lights at night so passengers could pick out their correct tram. The Addiscombe tram lights were red. The conductor could select the correct colour using a revolving disc above the end of the quarter lights. The rules for staff and passengers were strict:

Conductors must at all times while en route be active and attentive in the performance of their duties. They must neither sit nor lounge against the car or dash rail. Their entire time and attention is required in receiving passengers, providing seats, assisting elderly persons and children in getting in and out... politely attending to those who may wish to enter or leave the car...

THEY SHOULD MAKE EVERY ENDEAVOUR TO ACCOMMODATE THE PUBLIC.

And for passengers:

No person shall while travelling in or upon any carriage, play or perform any musical instrument. No person shall expectorate (spit) inside or outside any carriage. No person shall swear or use obscene language.

By 1909 the Addiscombe line benefited from four cars providing a service every ten minutes.

But then came the First World War. This had far-reaching implications for Croydon trams as for most other spheres of activity. So many men enlisted for service in the Army that the company was forced to employ women conductors. In those days it was almost inconceivable that a woman should do what was viewed as a man's work. The male employees went on strike in protest but within five weeks returned to work and the women were employed at the same rate as the men. With the conflict over, however, all the women conductors had been replaced by men by May 1919.

The Addiscombe line was very popular and the most profitable of the Croydon lines, but during the first World War both track and cars had not been adequately maintained. Deliberations about whether to renew the line or scrap it altogether started as early as 1919. It was not, however, until 1926, when the Commissioner of Police found the line to be dangerous, that the decision was made to stop the service.

Trolley buses were considered, but by then motor buses had become more reliable and this was considered to be the way forward.

R.I.P.

The last tram, Car No.70, commenced its final journey from Crown Hill on 31 March 1927 at 11.30p.m. The car was heavily draped and the Manager of The Royal Cinema provided a wreath. The packed car left to the rousing valedictions of a large crowd. Further crowds at the Leslie Arms hailed the passing of the tram. By the time it reached Addiscombe, there was a veritable throng of people. As the tram stopped, the crowd surged forward on to the car. The overladen vehicle began its ultimate journey to a chorus of clanging bells, and 'Auld Lang Syne'. Cycles and motorcars formed a lengthy cortège.

THE OMNIPOTENT OMNIBUS

The following morning heralded a new era. Addiscombe saw a very different kind of vehicle ranging over its roads. The London General Omnibus Company had placed in service the covered-top NS bus on route 178. This ran every four minutes from the Black Horse, Addiscombe to Crown Hill with a journey time of only 12 minutes. Since Cherry Orchard Road was being rebuilt, the 178 ran up Canning Road along with bus No. 2. Residents and shopkeepers in the Leslie Arms area protested at the lack of services and claimed they had been made 'April Fools'.

In December 1927 the London General Omnibus Company informed Croydon Corporation that the two Addiscombe routes, 197 and 178, were not profitable and the service was reduced. More protests followed. These were given public voice by the Addiscombe Branch of the Croydon Rate Payers Association whose members, no longer benefiting from the tram, resented subsidising the loss-making service to other parts of the borough. This was reported in the Croydon Times of 11 February 1928 in an amusing article, 'Driving Home the Thin End of the Wedge'. It is good to see that even then residents associations were making residents' views heard!

THE NEW ERA

And so in 2000 we experience the new era of the tram. What will unfold has yet to be seen. Croydon Tramlink is a new 28km light rail system, which uses disused and underused railway alignments around Croydon and links them together with some new sections to a street running in a loop around Central Croydon. Running from Wimbledon in the west through Croydon to New Addington, Beckenham and Elmers End in the east it does what most existing railways fail to do – it allows passengers direct East-West links without travelling via Central London and provides realistic alternatives to the car.

The trams used are Bombardier CR-4000 vehicles built at the BWS works in Vienna, Austria. Each tram can carry 200 people with 70 seated. The low floor design means that the tram and the platform edge are level and can easily be used by pushchair- and wheelchair-users and space for these is provided in each car.

The cars themselves are 30 metres long with an articulated 2-unit design, electrically powered via overhead wires at 750vdc. After much consultation, negotiation and argument, construction started in earnest in 1997 and although several problems delayed the opening by a few months, the first section to New Addington opened on 10th May 2000.

To connect Beckenham and Elmers End with Croydon, the system replaced the existing Elmers End to Addiscombe Railway (closed 31 May 1997) and the disused Woodside-Selsdon Railway (closed 13 May 1983). The stub to the original railway terminus at Addiscombe was closed permanently, and the new Addiscombe Tramstop was constructed between Bingham Road and Lower Addiscombe Road close to the old Bingham Road station on the Selsdon line (and just a short distance from the old terminus of Addiscombe's first Tramway!). To make the line more accessible, the old bridge abutments and embankments were removed and the line is now at ground level, crossing both roads under traffic-light control.

The route through Addiscombe to Beckenham opened on 23 May 2000 with the second route to Elmers End following a week later. The Tramlink system has already been a huge success and extensions must be on the cards in the future.

Modern-day tram crossing site of former Bingham Bridge, July 2000 (S.C.)

Tram No.65 by Bingham Bridge on last day of operation, 31 March 1927. (C.L.S.L.)

PLANES *by Steve Collins*

If the reader is wondering why we included planes in connection with Addiscombe, you might be interested to learn that, as the bi-plane flies, Croydon Airport is less than three miles away and grew to be a large employer of local people. It is not everyone that can boast the world's first International Airport virtually on their doorstep.

It all started in 1915 when the new Royal Flying Corps (later to become the RAF) defence station was formed alongside Plough Lane Beddington on New Barn Farm - formally part of the Carew Estates. This was to help protect the area from German Zeppelin bomb attacks (see Edwardian Addiscombe). In 1918, National Aircraft Factory No. 1 was built near by with its own airfield. The future King George VI gained his 'wings' there in 1919 with one of the training squadrons.

After the First World War, the Aerodrome expanded rapidly and was adopted as the Customs Airport of London in 1920 - which all made for lots of International comings and goings.

One of the first was KLM - the Dutch airline. Founded in 1919, they flew their first passenger service from Croydon to Amsterdam (Schipol) in 1920, later to be joined by Sabena (Belgium), Air France and Lufthansa.

Air transport was really taking off. Just think of the rapid innovation involved. From the Wright brothers having made their first powered flight at Kitty Hawk on 17 December 1903, through fighting aircraft just ten years later and International air passenger travel less than a decade after that.

But who were making these capable planes? At Croydon we had Handley Page (H.P.). After the war, Croydon Aerodrome was left with hangers full of spares and big bi-plane bombers. Seizing the opportunity, H.P. purchased the majority, and with an ace design team, refitted the bombers to make machines for the coming air transport age. They made HP 42s and HP 45s, the numbers reflecting the number of passengers that they could carry. All of the HP machines were named after Greek characters that

Peter J. Little in October 2000. Peter belongs to the Croydon Airport Society and is pictured here at the Communications Centre in the newly opened Airport museum. People interested in joining the Society should contact Tom Samson at 18 Great Woodcote Park, CR8 3QS. (C.A.)

began with an 'H' - Hercules, Helena, Hannibal, etc.

In 1924 Imperial Airways was formed from the independent British airline operators then using the aerodrome and it was the first time that the Government had offered investment monies.

The marvellous main terminal building (Airport House) was erected between 1926-28 on the newly built Purley Way, and opened in May 1928 by the Air Minister's wife.

It was here in the Control Tower that all the principles of modern air traffic control were devised by the talented Jimmy Jeffs, the two sons of whom are now intimately involved with the Croydon Airport Society. But more of this later.

Until the final Lufthansa departure on the last day of August 1939 (think about the date!), Croydon - or at least its airport - was the most glamorous place in Britain. The adjacent Aerodrome Hotel - another world first - sold roof space at a penny a head to people greeting the famous aviators of the time.

In 1927 when Charles Lindbergh dropped in with his monoplane Spirit of St Louis after the first non-stop flight between New York and Paris the crowd at Croydon was the largest ever seen at an airport. This was only subsequently equalled by the Beatles' return from America to Heathrow in 1963.

The airport's finest times were surely the 11 years between 1928-39. It was the world's first bespoke airport, and during this period remained the largest.

In 1932, Croydon Airport provided the six pence airletter (airmail) carrier service to anywhere in the world. This proved highly popular, particularly for commercial paperwork. The DH 42 & 45 'Silver Wing' flights from Croydon to Paris, and the reciprocal French 'Rayon d'Or' service proved most popular. But passenger air transport was expensive, and so was typically the prerogative of the rich and famous. To name but a few - Garbo, Chaplin, Douglas Fairbanks, James Stewart, Mary Pickford and Winston Churchill (who almost lost his life at the airport). To find out more about the airport, readers may wish to refer to the video 'Travellers in Time' available from the Croydon Airport Society.

⟫ Croydon ⟪
Airport & Imperial
Airways

Top left: *Croydon Airport in 1929 - an artist's illustration by Kenneth McDonough. The pilot was probably 'all-weather Mac'. Whilst the passengers were weather tight inside he would only fly in an open cockpit.*

Above: *Helena HP42 being prepared for departure in 1928.* (B.W.)

Top right: *Imperial Airways Poster, 1930.* (T.P./B.)

Right: *Imperial Airways airliner Hannibal HP42 over Croydon Airport, 1928.* (B.W.)

Below: *The main terminal building erected 1926-28.* (B.W.)

1928 Delivery of new HP42 to the airport and inspection. (B.W.)

Amy Johnson arrives back at Croydon Airport, August 1930. The crowds turn out to take advantage of the Aerodrome Hotel 'penny a head' roof top view. (C.A.)

AMY JOHNSON

Born in Hull in 1903, the wonderful Amy Johnson excelled in sports, got a degree from Sheffield University, had a very unhappy love affair with some Swiss stinker, and so moved to London to work as a secretary. Finding herself one day in Edgware, home of the London Aeroplane Club, she barged in and demanded lessons from an instructor.

In July 1929 she was awarded her 'A' pilots licence, had to do her own engineering repairs, became the first woman to gain a ground engineer's licence and was known as 'Johnny' in the hangers.

Amy wangled a second hand Gypsy Moth and flew it 150 miles to say tat-tah to her parents in Hull. And with that under her flying jacket, she got sponsorship from Castrol Oil and took off from Croydon in 1930 to make a solo flight to Darwin in Australia. Not daunted by the challenge, Amy did it and was dubbed 'the Queen of the Air'. Her Gypsy Moth was called 'Jason' – and it still exists. It hangs from the ceiling of the aviation gallery at the London Science Museum and a replica has recently been built by the Yorkshire Air Museum to commemorate her return to Croydon in August 1930. Tens of thousands crowded to the airport to greet her triumphant return.

With the advent of war, the airport closed for commercial traffic and became a strategic RAF Spitfire and Hurricane fighter base. With the relative adjacency of Kenley and Biggin Hill fighter airfields, Croydon became a prime target for the Luftwaffe bombing strategy.

On 15 August 1940, Croydon experienced its first Second World War air raid. And this was big, with over 1000 German bombers and fighters. The raiders attacked before the sirens were sounded. At Croydon Airport, 62 people were killed in the raid, 37 seriously injured and 137 slightly injured.

After the war, the airport reverted to its previous commercial operation, which quickly outgrew available space leading to the building of Gatwick in its place.

Croydon Airport finally closed on 30 September 1959 and was substantially redeveloped as housing estates. Still remaining is the lovingly restored Airport House main building which boasts some fine Art Deco detail. Outside is a Heron Aircraft - one of the last to leave the airport.

In October 2000 the Croydon Airport Preservation Society re-opened the Control Tower as a Museum. This is now open to the public on the first Sunday in every month.

*Amy Johnson in her famous 'Jason' Gypsy Moth,
1930. During the Second World War, Amy was
part of the Transport Auxillary. On 5 January
1941, whilst ferrying an Airspeed Oxford, in
heavy weather, she ran out of fuel over the
Thames Estuary.
She was just 38 years old, and her body was
never recovered. (B.W.)*

Croydon Airport August 1930. Amy gets mobbed after the return from her historic flight. (C.A.)

A.E. Clouston lands the twin engined DH mono plane Comet Racer 'Boomerang' in a record-breaking flight from Australia, via New Zealand, 1938. The Comet Racer had a huge light up its nose, which can be seen being inspected by an engineer. (C.A.)

This is probably Clouston and Victor Rickets returning to Croydon in the DH Comet Racer after shattering Amy Johnson's time to Cape Town, 1938. During the war, New Zealand born Clouston stayed in England and volunteered to check the effectiveness of the new Barrage Balloon wires. This was an incredibly risky task but through super piloting skills, he always got back to base. (C.A.)

Chapter 11
Addiscombe Schools

by Anne Bridge with grateful acknowledgement to Mrs L. Thornhill and Miss Jayne for notes on Oval School.

As we have seen, Croydon was the scene of rapid development during the second half of the 19th century, with the subsequent explosion in population. The housing and population varied considerably.

Bob Corner, c.1910. (B.C.)

In the more affluent areas there were a number of private schools of differing size and curriculum, depending on the type of students being taught. Education was seen as being mainly for boys, and girls were educated to a lesser degree. Boys destined for university and the liberal professions would have received a largely academic education at places such as Whitgift School. For those requiring a more practical education for their sons, Mr N.J. Lutte MCP advertised himself as 'Lecturer on History and Geography, Professor of Languages, etc'. From 1882 until 1900 he ran the Addiscombe Educational Institute, for most of that time at 3 Madeira Villas, Addiscombe Road, where Cheney Court now stands. He specialised in practical subjects, languages, book-keeping and other commercial subjects.

Even smaller, between 1878 and 1885, Miss B. Granger ran the Addiscombe Preparatory School for young ladies from No.1 St John's Villas, now known as 42 Canning Road.

Illustrated are Addiscombe New College on Lower Addiscombe Road and the Winton House School which for many years was a respected school and landmark on Addiscombe Road until its sudden closure. It has now been sympathetically and beautifully refurbished as the Ismaili Centre.

(J.G.)

Winton House School 1st XI 1932

Oval Road School, c.1910. (B.C.)

Coronation of Edward VII, Lower Addiscombe Road 1901. (C.L.S.L.)

Oval School

In 1870 an Education Act was passed 'to provide sufficient school accommodation for the whole infant population of the country and to make attendance of all children at school compulsory'. Consequently in 1871 the Croydon School Board was formed and on 29 September 1873 the Oval Road Board Schools were opened.

Life in those days was very different for the pupils of Oval Road School, as it was then known. There were four schools: Infants, Junior Mixed, Senior Girls and Senior Boys, each with its own head teacher. On the first day the Infants had 43 pupils, the Juniors 48, Senior Girls 6 and Senior Boys 46. Each school consisted of one classroom with one teacher (the head) with possible help from pupil teachers.

Pupils were expected to pay 1d. (one penny, known as school pence) per day but for many families, struggling to make ends meet, this was impossible. What's more it could be hard to encourage parents to send their older children to school as they were needed to earn extra money for the family or to look after younger siblings. To overcome this problem, pupils could attend either the day school or the evening school. The parents of pupils under a certain age were interviewed by the School Attendance Board before their children were allowed to attend the evening school. The same teachers ran the day as well as the evening school and you wonder how they had the energy!

Attendance was very much affected by the weather. Many more children then had inadequate footwear and clothing. From 1890 well-meaning people sent second-hand clothing to the school for those pupils who needed it. As clothes were therefore precious and had to last, the cap and bonnet rooms were kept locked. Ill health also affected attendance. In an era before mass vaccination and antibiotics, certain illnesses were far more prevalent with possibly serious or fatal consequences: measles, mumps, diphtheria, typhoid, ringworm and scarlet fever were recorded in the school log.

The classrooms were heated by a single coal fire which created a lot of dust. The head teachers complained about the inadequate cleaning of the classrooms. In the early days overcrowding was a problem but this was relieved by the opening of the Woodside Schools in 1891.

Pupil teachers could be as young as 13 or 14. They were put into a school on probation for a five-year apprenticeship, after which they ranked as trained but uncertified. To become certified they had then to attend Training College. Training pupil teachers formed part of the head teacher's duties. When stock was needed at the school, a pupil teacher accompanied by the biggest of the boys fetched the required items from the Croydon Education Office.

Inspectors had a significant role in the running of the school. Mrs Scott, head of the Infants from the school's opening until 1902, regularly received glowing reports: 'Her children are quiet, well-behaved and managed with exceeding good sense and kindliness'. In 1876 the report ends 'This promises to be one of the best Infant Schools in the district'.

The curriculum was determined by the Inspectors, although head teachers could introduce subjects with the Inspectors' permission. Cookery was considered acceptable for the girls but Mrs Howse, head of the Girls' School, was summoned before the Schools Management Committee in July 1889 and ordered to stop teaching her pupils French as this was training the girls above their station! Subjects included maths, English, music and elementary science. Shorthand, still fairly new, was taught from 1893.

Mr Watson, the third head teacher of the Boys' School, was the first to enter boys for the Whitgift School examination. In 1892 four out of five free places offered by Whitgift went to Oval Road boys.

When the Oval Road School first opened, there were four fixed holidays: two weeks at Christmas, two weeks at Easter, one week at Whitsun and three weeks at Harvest. Many families went hop-picking resulting in absences at the beginning of the autumn term. In addition extra days were granted for special occasions, such as prize giving and a whole week break plus half a day for sports at Duppas Hill for the Coronation of Edward VII (*opposite, bottom*).

From 1900 to the First World War the staff were well qualified and Inspectors' reports enthusiastic. Oval Road pupils gained a high proportion of scholarships at Whitgift, Whitgift Middle, Selhurst, Old Palace and Stanley schools.

By now overcrowding had again become a problem along with a lack of adequate heating and the general state of the buildings.

On 13 October 1915 one of the very first Zeppelin bombs to fall in Croydon landed on one of the offices in the corner of the boys' playground. Most of the school's glass was shattered and already crumbling ceilings fell in. The school was not re-opened until early November.

The First World War brought staff shortages as teachers signed up for service. The Oval Road School knew the same tragedy that many others experienced. Mr Bottomley, who was aged 26 and had been teaching at the school for three years, was killed on 30 September in the Aisne battle. Mr S.A. Creek signed up in August and was killed in the Battle of the Somme. On 8 April 1918 the schools received the news that the head teacher, Sydney Beaumont, had died in France; he was a well-loved and dedicated

Oval School suffered damage at the hands of a zeppelin on 13 October 1915. (C.L.S.L.)

Former Winton School, now the Ismaili Centre, July 2000. (A.B.)

teacher. A tablet incorporated in the present school commemorates the names of master and former pupils who gave their lives during the First World War. Daylight raids began in 1917 so air-raid drill was practiced. When air raids led to low attendance rates, the school was closed. After the war there were a number of staffing shortages but things began to look up when Mr J.P. George became the head teacher in the autumn of 1922. Mr George was described as a real gentleman and born leader. He took part in the 1908 Olympics in the 220 metres. He would leave the school promptly at 4.00p.m. on a Friday and travel at his own expense to such places as Amsterdam, Liege and Antwerp to take part in athletic meetings. He tried hard three times to secure better playing fields for the school but with no success.

Problems with the building continued until 1931 when during the summer holiday the old building was demolished. The new building, as it stands today, was costly because the school was built on a former gravel site and required particularly deep foundations. As various parts of the building were completed, the school re-opened in stages during the autumn of 1931. The new building was designed to house the Senior School on the upper floor and the Junior and Infants Schools, along with the domestic science and handicraft rooms for the Senior School, on the ground floor.

The Second World War brought much disruption. On 4 September 1939 a large number of children and mothers were evacuated to Brighton. Some returned that winter whilst the others remained. In effect that meant there were two Oval Schools running at the same time, one in Addiscombe and one in Brighton. From August 1940 onwards the logbooks of both schools record frequent air raids with teachers and children taking refuge in shelters. The last air-raid alarm for a while was recorded on 8 May 1941 and the schools settled down not to be disrupted again until the flying bomb and rocket attacks during the summer of 1944.

When the 1944 Education Act came into force, the Senior School closed and the Primary School of 14 classes occupied the whole building, and in 1949

two schools, Infants and Juniors, occupied the same site. Paul Nihill (see Local Heroes) attended the school.

Immediately after the war there was no canteen at the school so every day at 12.15p.m. the teaching staff and dinner ladies conducted all the children to the Civic Restaurant in Lower Addiscombe Road. This was no mean feat. The line of children stretched almost the length of Cherry Orchard Road with pupils dodging round shoppers and open stalls full of tempting apples and other produce. When it rained, the pupils had to sit and eat in wet clothes and, by time they had made the return journey, they were even wetter.

The school had no hot water and no covered way to the (unlit) toilets. Some pupils were afraid of the gloom in the loos. There was no drinking water available. The new head teacher of Infants, Miss Jayne (head teacher between 1949 and 1966), commenced a long and determined fight for improved conditions, which she ultimately saw effected. Miss Jayne evidently achieved much for the school but in her reminiscences pays handsome tribute to the hardworking staff, dinner ladies and supportive parents.

It is clear from the way past pupils speak of the school, that they have many fond memories.

Above right and right:
Addiscombe New College, Lower Addiscombe Road corner Nicholson Road, c.1921. (J.G.)

Ashburton Library which stands on the site of the former Stroud Green House which has a chequered past. Owners included (1869-78) Henry Dorling, who raced horses at Woodside Racecourse. It was then bought by a priest who intended to turn it into a monastery. Lavish building plans were not completed and the library is now housed in what used to be the chapel. (J.G.)

The former Addiscombe Picture Palace. From 1910 until 1917 No. 13 Cherry Orchard Road was the only cinema that Addiscombe possessed. There were 132 seats at 2d. each with a non-stop programme from 3p.m. until 10.30p.m. Children were admitted at half price on Saturdays. The old projection booth is in the gap between the buildings.

Chapter 12
Entertainment

by Isha Shona Gabrielle, Steve Collins and Paul Nihill

WOODSIDE RACECOURSE
by Isha Shona Gabrielle

I am a pupil at Ashburton Community School in Shirley. In April 2000, I was asked whether I would like to write about the fact that my school was built on Woodside Race Course. I thought this would be a great opportunity to find out about the history of Ashburton and that it would be fun to do the research with my friend.

The first races in Croydon were at Park Hill but there were complaints about the state of the grounds. Because of its financial success, the Race Committee endeavoured to find a new venue. On 27 November 1866, Stroud Green, Woodside, now known as Shirley Road, became the new site for the race course and the Racing Committee signed a 14-year contract. Ashburton Community School was built on part of the Woodside Racecourse. The racecourse was, apparently, very attractive and had 13 or 14 obstacles, most of them natural.

The actual site of the course ran from Long Lane to Long Lane Wood in the north and Chaffinch Brooke in the south east. Most of this area is now the Ashburton Community School site.

The course was right handed and was one mile and 660 yards long with a gentle turn about half a mile out. It then became fairly straight, heading south west. A quarter of a mile before the winning post there was a rigid climb which tested the horses' stamina. The winning post itself was on a chute which ended near Stroud Green Road. The subsoil of the area was clay and this resulted in the course tending to be heavy going. Depending on the reports read, the course was all or partially grass. A prominent part of the new course was the Great Water Jump opposite the stand, often called the 'sensation' water jump. It was 15 feet long and wider than the one used in the Grand National. It was difficult to jump over the brook because the furze fence that guarded it was very tall, about five feet. The horses had to tackle the water jump at a fast enough pace to clear the brook. The fences contributed to several casualties and gave rise to a lot of complaints. The fence after the winning post had a noticeable drop in height and length due to the poor ground there. It was the cause of many disasters!

The first race on the new course was the South Country Hunt Cup, which featured a few accidents amongst the four runners but the feat was won by Fred Hobson on his mount, Bishopton, by 20 lengths. Henry Dorling, who lived nearby in Stroud Green House, raced at Woodside during the 1870s. He was the step-father of Isabella Mayson, by then married as Mrs Beeton the famous cookery book writer. Many important races had their beginnings at Woodside, such as the Grand Metropolitan Steeplechase and the Croydon Hurdle Race. Fred Archer was one of the famous jockeys who often rode there.

In 1871 the railway station at Woodside opened to improve transport to the course. The racecourse closed on 29 November 1890 and the races were transferred to Gatwick. After its closure the land was used for allotments and the Beckenham Golf Course. In 1950, Ashburton School, named after Lady Ashburton who formerly owned the estate, was built on part of the site. The school was known as 'Cashburton' by local residents because of the high cost of the building. The first head teacher of Ashburton Secondary Boys' School was Mr C.J. Stone, and Miss J. Joyce was the head teacher of the Girls' School. In 1970 the schools became mixed, with Mr G. Manning as the head teacher.

ADDISCOMBE CRICKET CLUB *by Steve Collins*

It was Canning Road, built on the Croydon side of the former (East India Company) estate, that provided the first home for Addiscombe Cricket Club when it was first formed in 1866. The ground occupied a pleasant rural setting at the rear of where the Addiscombe St Mary Magdalen Parish Church now stands. Only half a mile distant was the Cricketers Inn, still in business at the time of writing.

Only limited records of the Club exist from those early days, but it was obviously a strong one, fielding two elevens with matches being played against clubs as far afield as Putney - and even the Surrey County team. The club attracted and encountered some extraordinary players - the record breaking Crawford family to name just several.

In 1905 the stumps were finally pulled at the Canning Road ground to make way for building development. At the same time, another club in the area - Ashburton - had to vacate their ground next to Ashburton Road. The Ashburton Cricket Club had been fortunate enough to find another ground on part of Woodbury Farm in Radcliffe Road - less than half a mile south of the Cricketers Inn.

With the enforced closure of the original Addiscombe Cricket Club, the Ashburton Club adopted its name, poached some of the Addiscombe players, and a second Addiscombe Cricket Club came into being. The new ground was not the one that the club plays on today. In fact, at this time Radcliffe Road terminated where the tunnel of the then Brighton & South Coast Railway cutting crossed. Many a ball was lost in the cutting!

Whilst all of this had been going on, and with the departure from the Canning Road ground, a group of enthusiastic youngsters, connected with St Mary Magdalen Church, banded together under the leadership of the vicar - Revd A.B. Taylor - to form their own club. And it was this little club that was responsible for Addiscombe Cricket Club as it exists today.

The years of the First World War obviously took their toll on player numbers and the interest in the game, but in 1924 it all came together again. A new ground was needed, and to answer the committee's prayer, Sheed Thompson & Co announced that they were giving up the tenancy of a ground just to the east of the Creed (See Local Heroes) practice ground in Radcliffe Road. In negotiations with the Whitgift Foundation, it all came to pass. The current Sandilands site was finally purchased in 1925, amalgamated with the Radcliffe Road Tennis Club, and became 'The Addiscombe Cricket and Lawn Tennis Club'. With a new pavilion, proper groundsmen and equipment, the club went from strength to strength.

Addiscombe Cricket Club flourished, gained a superb reputation for its high standards and good hospitality - particularly their excellent social functions. All of this attracted the big players to the grounds.

To have players of the calibre of Subba Row, Lock and Dexter (to name but a few) batting and balling with you says something. Some 10 years back I seem to recall seeing Addiscombe scoring a super six against the MCC (editor). The excellent 1990 book *Addiscombe Cricket Club - A History* by Peter Stanley Williams, will tell you a lot more.

Top: Addiscombe Cricket Club 1926.
Centre: *Addiscombe Cricket Club 1932.*
Standing: S. Pierce, Allon Taylor, Lee Flux, S. Roe; seated, Hayes, Horlick, Woodhouse, H.E. Pierce, Hinton, Geary, Bullock; in front: Yewlett.
Bottom: *Addiscombe v An England XI, Sandilands 11 September 1960.*
Left to right, standing: H. Pierce, A. Goddard, C. Dring, D. Oliver, M. Woodhouse, L.Pullen, A Fletcher, M. Burrows, W. Bower, M. Williams, P. Barnes, F. Harris, A. Oliver, R. Houghton, M. Smith, T. Greenhough, A. Allen, D. Padgett, A Woodhouse; seated: P. Richardson, R. Subba Row, F. Tyson, R. Swetman, A. Moss, G. Lock, E. Dexter.

Paul Nihill (centre) in 1951 with David Deller and Albert Jeal (left foreground) and Evans, Robinson and Nicholls (centre back).

SIR PHILIP GAME BOYS' CLUB
by Paul Nihill

On 19 July 1947 the then Home Secretary Mr J. Chuter Ede opened the Sir Philip Game Boys' Club at 'The Cedars', 38 Morland Avenue. The club was named after Air Vice-Marshall Sir Philip Game, GCB, GCVO, GBH, KCMG, DSO. When I was enrolled as a member in September 1950, the club offered endless facilities for its young members. On the sporting side you could choose from athletics, bicycle polo, billiards/snooker, boxing, cricket, football, gymnastics, judo, table tennis and tennis – there being several outdoor courts.

For the less energetic you could participate at any of the following: art (which my mother ran), car maintenance or the concert party where as a teenager Roy Hudd got his first experience on the stage. There were also metal, plastic and woodwork classes and even a shoe-repair class, which in those days was very useful indeed. I've no doubt forgotten a couple of activities but by now you have surely got the picture of just how much the club could offer its members and why it was so very popular.

The local Police at Z Division encouraged and participated in several of the club's activities and sometimes if a kid got into trouble the Police would encourage him to join Sir Philip Game Boys' Club.

My two chief interests at the time were athletics and boxing and I eagerly joined both sections. I was just eleven years of age, the required age to join the club and I never looked back. They were wonderful days. It was open five nights a week and there was always a queue outside at 6.30p.m. when the warden Mr Rourke opened up.

The boxing section produced several amateur champions that went on to win major titles in the professional ranks. The famous McKenzie brothers, Brian Brazier, Frankie Lucas and, though not a local lad, a certain Frank Bruno were amongst the champions that trained in the first-class gymnasium.

I was a sprinter in those days never tackling more than 220 yards. One day the Assistant Warden Mr Pat Maloney persuaded me to run in the Croydon Youth Cross-Country Championship over three miles at Addington. To me this was like running to the end of the earth. Not wishing to embarrass myself I trained for the event and aimed at a place in the first 30. Running against boys of up to two years older than me I astonished myself and others by finishing third and helping the club to win the team title. After that I concentrated on the longer distance events which was to prove to be my forté in athletics. I owe a great deal to the late Pat Maloney.

In 1952 the David Deller Hall was built. This excellent building was named after the club Chairman and served as a first-class gymnasium and hall of entertainment. One of the annual highlights was always the club pantomime produced by Doris Cooper on behalf of the club's concert party. I can still picture Roy Hudd singing and clowning his way through the shows. I was one of his principal guests on the occasion of the television showing of his 'This is Your Life' several years ago. The club had a wonderful cheap canteen where you could buy a large mug of delicious drinking chocolate for just one penny. When I was broke – which in those days was often – I'd borrow a couple of pence from Roy to spend in the canteen.

Lord Mountbatten of Burma visited the club in the early 1950s during which time he presented me with a fountain pen for my athletics. My Mum killed herself with laughter when I told her, 'Mountbatten, you must be dreaming again' she said. A week later a photograph of his visit was in the local newspaper.

The club would give exhibitions of gymnastics and judo at local fêtes and fairs. The standard was always very high thanks to the leadership of Pat Maloney (gymnastics) and Harry Harding (judo).

One of the club's most dismal sporting failures ever occurred back in 1955 when they were surprisingly beaten 32-2 in the 1st round of the Croydon Youth Football Cup at Purley Way by a church youth group team (St Margaret's). In goal - me! Our trainer, Sgt Crump of the Z Division Police, said afterwards 'Nihill, you might make an athlete one day but you'll never be a bloody footballer'. Incidentally one of our two goals was scored by the referee who felt sorry for us! His name - Wally Male, my stepfather.

In the late forties and fifties several charity football matches were played at Selhurst Park (Crystal Palace FC) in aid of Sir Philip Game Boys' Club and involved some of the greatest footballers this country has ever seen. One of the games in 1949 attracted over 27 000 fans. That's more than Crystal Palace get today in Division One. Today the club is still there but is no longer a boys' club but a recreation centre. You'll never better Sir Philip Game Boys' Club as it once was; it was truly a great club. Thousands of kids must have passed through the doors of 'The Cedars' in its time and I was one of them.

Above and right: *The bomb site corner of Warren Road and Lower Addiscombe Road in the 1950s* (C.L.S.L.) *and in August 2000 with Warren Court and the corner of Threshers wine store.* (S.C.)

Left: *Paul's brothers and friends. At the front: Alan Male; in the middle, second from left is John Critchley whose family owned the greengrocers shop at No. 93 Lower Addiscombe Rd. Second from the right in the middle is Andy Male and on the right next to him is a boy named Brown whose family owned another greengrocers shop at No.115 Lower Addiscombe Rd.* (P.N.)

Opposite: *Paul outside the Alma.* (P.N.)

Chapter 13
Local Heroes

by Paul Nihill, Vic Cheal, Steve Collins,
Barbara Broughton and Anne Bridge

PAUL NIHILL MBE

Paul Nihill was Addiscombe and Croydon's first ever Olympic medallist. In 1964 he won a silver medal in Tokyo for the 50km walk. During a distinguished athletics career he has held world records for the 3km and 5km track and the 20km and 30km road walks. He is a former member of the Sir Philip Game Boys' Club. Now living in the Medway area, Paul Nihill still plays an active role in local sports clubs. In 1976 he was awarded the MBE for services to sport. Born in 1939, Paul records his memories of living in Addiscombe...

I moved into 109a Lower Addiscombe Road with my mother, Margaret Rose Nihill, either late in 1943 or early in 1944. It was to be our first real home. Previously we had lived in South Croydon and Kenley. I was actually born in Colchester, Essex, but left there as a baby. No.109a was at the time over an empty shop. It was war time and one of my first memories of living there was huddling up close to my mother in the cold, damp cellar in the summer of 1944 when Hitler began his V1 flying bomb (doodlebug) assault on Britain. Fortunately none fell too close to us.

Previously we had sought the safety of the local air-raid shelter which was situated on the right hand side of Addiscombe Station. A short while later we acquired a Morrison shelter supplied free by the Borough Engineer's Office. A Morrison shelter is best described as a steel-topped cage in which you slept. Should the house cave in, you would be safe from the falling debris. We kept this in the back of the shop. Incidentally, when not in use, the shelter would double as a table.

I was too young to be fearful of the war, though I knew when the air-raid siren went off everyone would run for cover. It was a sound once heard you never forgot.

In September of 1944 I started school at Woodside Infants and even at the tender age of five used to make my own way there on foot via Grant Place, Highbarrow and Coniston Roads. It was at Lower Addiscombe Road that I was first aware of life around me. The shops and the people became part of my life. I have to admit here that my memory of the area has been greatly helped by reference to a 1946 Croydon Directory which has enabled me to be precise when listing names and numbers. If we go back to the period at the end of the war, 1945/46, and take a stroll along past the shops from Warren Road to Grant Road, we'd find a far different scene to that of today.

We had a great selection of shops in those days; the only one missing was a fish and chip shop. To get your fourpence (2p) worth of chips you had to either pop up past the Leslie Arms public house or pop down to Bingham Halt (now Addiscombe tram stop but originally there was a railway station with a bridge over the road there).

Warren Road Before we start our shop-to-shop tour, let me tell you about the large bomb patch at the top of Warren Road (at the intersection with Lower Addiscombe Road) where Warren Court now stands. Before the bomb fell on 19 April 1941, six shops had stood on that stretch including The Cosy Restaurant, Perkins the grocers, A. Parkins – Tailor, and Bishops Tobacconist. The bomb site was a great play area, as all the local bomb patches were, and I will always remember Guy Fawkes Night. For weeks kids would prepare by collecting everything they could lay their hands on that would burn. By the time the big night came, we had a bonfire [that was] second to none. It was always a great occasion.

Just a few doors down Warren Road on the same side as the bomb patch was Mrs Frances Dalton's small general store which has long since closed.

Lower Addiscombe Road   Nos.85-99 were known in Victorian times as Sydney Terrace; No.85 was Addiscombe Wine & Spirit Stores. When we were young, we used to raid their back yard for empty beer bottles which we then took into the shop and cheekily claimed 2d. (1p) a bottle. In those days there was a bottle shortage and on certain bottles you had to pay a deposit. Three bottles returned was equal to one week's pocket money.

No.87 [was] Whybrows the newsagent. This has always been in my living memory a newspaper shop. No.89 [was] George T. Ray - Optician, No.91 [was] Eric Remington - Confectioners & Tobacconist. No.93 [was] Ernie and Mabel Critchley's greengrocers. We were very friendly with the Critchleys. I remember them moving in some time in 1946. No.95 [was] Mr Rowe's Hardware Store. Mr Rowe was a white-haired gentleman who served the area well for years. As a young teenager he was always repairing my bike. When the paraffin heater craze was on, he would sell paraffin at one shilling (5p) a gallon. No.97 [was] Wimbles - the shoe repairers. I remember Mr Wimble only having one leg. My chum, Bill Walsh, lived above the shop and as a young lad was Broomfield's Baker's boy on a horse-drawn cart. He used to always shout to rival, Price's boy, 'Price's bread is made of lead. When you eat it you fall dead!' No.99 [was] William Clark's butchers.

Hastings Road At the top of Hastings Road on the left hand side walking down, at No.1 was an old 18th-century cottage, Heath Lodge, where it was rumoured the famous highwayman, Dick Turpin, once stayed the night. This was an historic building but in the 1950s and '60s the authorities seemed to delight in knocking down such buildings - a shame.

Next door to the cottage, at 3/5, were the Bowe Brothers (motor engineers). A few doors down at 11/13 were W. Gratwick & Sons - decorators and undertakers, which to me seems a strange combination.

Lower Addiscombe Road   Nos.101-113 were known in Victorian times as Canning Terrace. No.101 was Harry Leppard Ltd. - Wine & Spirit Merchants. At No.103 were Frank & Gwen Bury - Newsagents. My mother was very friendly with the Burys and used to work part-time for them. In the early fifties I used to do a morning and evening paper round for 15 shillings a week. Out of this I had to pay my mother housekeeping and buy most of my clothes, which were not surprisingly all secondhand bought from Mrs Williams who had a

shop nearby in 'Bang-Ole' which had a reputation for being a very tough area. When I think back now about what I wore in those days, I shudder. I must have looked ruddy awful but to be honest so did most of the kids.

No.105 was Harris & Bailey - Coal Merchants. Their horse-drawn carts were a familiar sight on the streets of Addiscombe. The stables were at the back of Number 111, in Hastings Place. Living next door to the stables I often used to pop in and see the huge horses which were often to be seen in big parades.

No.107 was T. Pearcy - Confectioners & Tobacconist. Two old ladies ran this most unfashionable shop that must have been a throw back to Victorian times. In those days of rationing we weren't able to buy very many sweets. I remember the two ladies being attacked and robbed by an intruder. They closed up soon after this shocking incident.

No.109 was Easton & Sons - Upholsterers, and from 1947-48 Bill Halswell - Motor Cycles. The shop was empty when we moved in. The upholsterers could only have been there a short while. When Bill Halswell acquired this shop, he retained his motor cycle shop at No.111. Over Bill's shop lived Hilda Sirett, one of the characters of the block. I used to look out the back window of our house and listen to her telling off her cat because it wouldn't go out and work for his living. She used to get very angry if people called her Mrs Syrup. She was an eccentric old dear.

No.113 was the Post Office. Like Whybrow's, the newsagents, this has in my living memory always been a Post Office. The Dare family lived over the shop.

Addiscombe Station   This building should never ever be demolished. For me this is Addiscombe's chief landmark. When the station opened, it was known as Croydon (Addiscombe Road). The road part of the title was dropped in 1925 and up until 1955 it was known as Addiscombe (Croydon). In June 1955 it became what we know it as today - Addiscombe Station.

Nos.115-129 were known in Victorian times as Regent Terrace. At No.115 was R. Brown the greengrocer. Outside this shop, next to the station and adjacent to the pavement was the air-raid shelter. The entrance had a sloping roof with the shelter below ground level. I remember it being knocked down and filled in. At No.117 was Willis & Co.'s Radio Shop. No.119 was Thomas M. Booth's chemists. With Mr Booth on the block you hardly needed a doctor for he would nearly always be able to prescribe a medicine to suit your needs.

No.121 was Ellis & Sons Furnishers. Mr Smith ran the Enterprise Café. I don't remember the furnishers but I do remember the cafe which in the 1950s had a juke-box which I always used to play. I cannot identify the shop at No.123. No.125 was Thomas & Castle the bakers. No.127 was F.J. Bennett the grocers and then Moore's the grocers. I always knew the above shop to be Moore's. We would do most of our weekly shopping here. These premises are now part of the extension to the Alma public house.

No.129 was the Alma Public House of William H. Webb. This was one place I did not frequent in the old days. I had to wait until I was 18 before I got my first drink there. Outside was a wooden type horse trough which was removed many years ago.

On the other side of Lower Addiscombe Road directly opposite the Alma, at the bottom of Clyde Road, was a large detached house that had a tower. To my knowledge it had always been empty. As kids in the late 1940s we'd spend hours playing in the house but, once night fell, we believed it to be haunted. We would dare anyone to enter the house on their own, climb the stairs to the tower and wave from the window. I don't remember any of us accepting the dare!

Directly opposite where we lived at the bottom right hand side of Canning Road was a branch of Barclays Bank. Further along in the stretch between Canning Road and Leslie Park Road was the old Methodist Church. Late one night on 21 January 1948 my mum woke me and said, 'The Methodist Church is on fire.' This was situated almost opposite us and I stayed up most of the night watching it being destroyed. It was a huge fire. Arson by a teenage gang was suspected but no one was ever caught.

Prior to the fire I used to attend Sunday School there. During the two years it took to build a new church, worshippers used a church in Canning Road which is no longer with us. Those who attended Sunday School used the annex of the church, the entrance of which was in Clyde Road (and which today is known as Clyde Hall). Continuing along Lower Addiscombe Road towards Leslie Park Road until we are opposite the top of Warren Road, we find at No.98 Wisby (Croydon) Ltd., a building contractors.

Next door at No.100 was the company Turners Transport Ltd., the removal people. Some time in the 1950s, Turners' site was taken over by L.J. Dove Ltd. who had a garage and car showrooms on it.

My mother was a local artist and in September 1952, then known as Mrs Margaret Male,

Right and above: *The 1956 Exhibition of Art by Children of the Commonwealth* (P.N.) *and Margaret Male, Paul's mother, at the exhibition, 21 September.* (C.T.)

formed the Addiscombe Children's Art Group which she ran for several years in our front room on the first floor. She organised many children's art exhibitions, including a Commonwealth one that had exhibits from all over the world. The group became very well known and would enter many competitions nationwide.

Sport At the top of Morland Avenue was Morland Park which had a lake on the estate. The Sir Philip Game Boys' Club, which opened in 1947, occupies part of the land. Roy Hudd, the comedian, and Clinton and Duke McKenzie, the champion boxers, were members. In 1951/52 I became a member of the Sir Philip Game Boys' Club. I at once joined the boxing section where the trainer was Albert Jeal. I wasn't exactly over active as a boxer but I did box right up until 1961.

I was a better athlete than boxer and this is the sport I concentrated on, though quite often I would combine the two. My local sporting heroes were Albert Finch, Mark Hart, Ron Pudney and Crystal Palace Football Club.

I have confined my memories to the direct vicinity in which I lived over 50 years ago. Despite moving away from Croydon 25 years ago, I have always regarded myself as an Addiscombe boy. It was my first real home and it is the place which I grew up in.

Top left: *Woodside Firefighters receiving breathing apparatus in Kings Avenue, Brixton 1944.* (A.Bo.)

Top right: *Woodside Firefighters. Does anyone know who the little girl is?* (C.T.)

Inset vignette: *Alma Boxhall as a baby. Alma's father was a Woodside Firefighter.* (A.Bo.)

Above: *Woodside Firefighters again.*

Above left: *Home Office demonstration bomb at Woodside Fire Station, 20 April 1938.* (C.A.)

Above and right: *St John's Ambulance, probably at Addiscombe Station and St Mildred's Church respectively.* (J.G. and C.A.)

FREDERICK GEORGE CREED

A former distinguished Addiscombe resident was Frederick George Creed, the inventor of the Creed High Speed Telegraph System and the Creed Teleprinter. Mr Creed was born in Mill Village, Nova Scotia, in October 1871 and he spent his early working life with the Western Union Telegraph and Cable Company. During this time he became self taught on the subject of cable and land-line telegraphy.

In 1890 he moved to New York where he worked firstly as a land-line morse operator before joining the Central and South American Telegraph and Cable Company as a cable operator until 1896. During this period he found the existing practice of transmitting signals by hand punching codes to be a laborious exercise. He suspected that letters and figures could be transmitted more easily by a machine based on the working principle similar to that of a typewriter.

In 1897 he moved to Scotland where, with the aid of a £300 grant from a local steel manufacturer, he developed a machine described as the Keyboard Perforator. His efforts came to the attention of Lord Kelvin, who after some initial reservations gave him full support. After producing morse prototypes in 1902, his work attracted the attention of the General Post Office who placed an initial order for 12 machines. After experiencing some early operating difficulties, in 1903 he produced the first reperforator receiver and in 1904 the Creed Morse Printer. Later that year he opened a small factory in Glasgow where he remained until 1909, when, along with some skilled mechanics, he moved to Selsdon Road in South Croydon.

Initial orders were received from the Eastern Telegraph Company and the Great Northern Cable Company based in Denmark. By 1912 the company employed a workforce of 72 men, and during the year, following successful field trials, the Creed Telegraph System was installed between the London and Manchester offices of the Daily Mail. Four other provincial newspapers took up the idea but further developments in the field were halted due to the outbreak of the First World War.

With the increasing demands of wartime, the business outgrew the Selsdon Road premises and in 1913 moved to the corner of Addiscombe and Cherry Orchard Roads, the site of a roller-skating rink, where it remained until 1966 when the business closed.

Following the end of the war work, the telegraph system resumed and in 1919 a series of demonstrations were successfully conducted before representatives from the newspapers and directors of the Press Association, the outcome being that other news agencies and provincial newspapers introduced the system. In 1923 the Creed Direct Printer was brought into operation and adopted for general use by the Post Office.

During 1928 Frederick Creed retired and the company was taken over by the International Telephone and Telegraph Company of America, the European controlling body being the Standard Telephone and Cable Company Ltd.

Frederick Creed has been described as having been of a strong and religious nature. The company remained very much under his personal control and it is said that all of the workers had to be non-smokers and that each had to sign a pledge not to drink alcohol.

In 1957 Creed was admitted as a Freeman of the City of London and shortly afterwards he died at the age of 86. For many years, and up to the time of his death, he had resided at 20 Outram Road, Addiscombe, with his wife, and a blue plaque commemorating the fact can be seen on the front wall of the house.

Top: *George Frederick Creed* (C.L.S.L.)

Above: *Creed's house in Outram Road.* (S.C.)

Right: *Plaque, Outram Road, representing Creed's contribution to the telegraph and teleprinting.* (S.C.)

The Pumping Station & Water Tower

Above: *Pumping Station in Stuarts Yard (off Surrey Street) before the listed building was restored in 1998.*

Right: *Water Tower at Park Hill, August 2000.*

Below: *Stuarts Yard Pumping Station after external restoration, August 2000.* (All photographs this page S.C.)

William Sturgeon was a great scientist who invented most of the useful devices as we know them today - items such as the battery, generator and electric motor. Born in Whittington, Lancashire, in 1783, Sturgeon was apprenticed to a shoe maker. In 1804 he enlisted in the Royal Artillery and at that time devoted his leisure time to scientific studies - particularly those connected with the then new science of electro-magnetism.

In 1824 Sturgeon was appointed Lecturer in Science and Philosophy at The East India College in Addiscombe. In 1824 he published four papers on the subject of electro and thermo electricity, and in 1825 was awarded the Silver Medal by the Society of Arts (now RSA) along with a purse of 30 guineas for his inventions. This provided him with the currency to make the first portable reliable battery, blow Faraday out of the water, and then proceed to design electric generators and motors.

Sturgeon also invented many other handy things - like lightning conductors for ships - which were of great use to the East India Company.

Its interesting to note that one of our other local technical heroes, Creed, would not have been able to make his teleprinters without Sturgeon's super inventions.

Baldwin Latham (1837-1917) was an excellent engineer and a true local hero who was fundamental in providing a safe water supply and sanitation for our area. In 1848 is was reckoned that 36.6 per cent of the Croydon mortality rate could have been avoided had a proper water supply and sewage disposal scheme been implemented. A Public Health Act was applied to Croydon on 1 August 1849 and in January 1850, an application was made to the General Board of Health to borrow the money for the necessary works. At the end of the day, the local Board managed to borrow some £196 000, repayable over a 30-year period.

There was a very good water supply in Sturt's Yard (just off Surrey Street/Scarbrook Road), and beneath in the chalk, it was believed that there was 'an ever flowing copious supply of water'. The site was purchased by a Mr G. Price, one of the then members of the Board. The tenants did not know that they were dealing with a Public Board, and the whole of the property, with possession, was acquired very cheaply.

But how to abstract the water? It would need a powerful pump. Someone - and we do not know who - had a moment of inspiration. Just down the road at West Croydon was an almost purpose-built pumping station, no longer in use, and up for sale by the Brighton Railway Company. Indeed, the pumping station was that which had been used to power the Croydon Atmospheric Railway! What a wonderful turn of the wheels! Purchased for just £250, the station was dismantled brick by brick in 1851, and rebuilt over the wells in Sturt's Yard. Re-equipped with two Cornish steam-pump engines, Croydon was on tap for potable water.

To distribute it, a reservoir was needed and the Local Board of Health (believe it not), along with the Archbishop of Canterbury, selected Park Hill Farm as an ideal spot being some 293ft above sea level. One acre was purchased for £100 in 1851, and work commenced in creating a huge underground reservoir of some 950 000 gallon capacity.

On 11 December 1851, the Archbishop of Canterbury started the pumps at what is now known as Sturt's Yard and drove to the new reservoir. Soon after his arrival came the first stream of water. In fact, it got there through a 12" main which passed along Mint Walk, Barclay Road and a special aqueduct near the end of Chatsworth Road. This was all good and fine, but with explosive demand for water in the Addiscombe and adjacent areas due to new housing development in the early 1860s, the reservoir could not provide sufficient pressure.

Baldwin Latham had been flushing around Croydon sanitation for some while. As a young 22 year old engineer he was hired as a Board consultant, and wrote copious technical reports in the 1858/62 period. In 1863 he was appointed as the surveyor for Croydon in such mucky matters. Apart from designing all of the new sewer systems, he gave our area proper water pressure and an enduring landmark in the form of the Park Hill water tower. Latham argued that - in the spirit of the Atmospheric Railway architects - all buildings should be 'grand'. And he got away with it - good for him! In 1870, Latham set up his own private practice, lived at Park Hill House, and until his death in 1917 in Havelock Road.

Park Hill water tower and reservoir. Filling up at the auxiliary pumps, 1937.
(C.A.)

GEOFFREY MOIR

Here are the four things I noticed within the first 30 seconds of meeting Geoffrey Moir: an impressive handlebar moustache, a warm smile, a bone-crushing handshake and a wonderful twinkle in the eye.

Flight Lieutenant Geoffrey Moir DFC and Bar is nearly 80 years old. He was born in Portland Road and moved to 37 Spring Lane when he was four years old. Geoffrey attended Addiscombe New College, which used to stand on the corner of Nicholson Road and the Lower Addiscombe Road, and then Croydon Boys' High School. As a boy he used to play tennis with his mother at the tennis club near Woodside Baptist Church where his grandmother provided the teas.

In 1941 Geoffrey Moir was employed by the Croydon Gas Company and that year joined the Air Force until he was demobilised in 1946. After training in Canada and the USA he joined Pathfinder Force of Bomber Command initially with the 19th Squadron then 97 Squadron based. Guy Gibson, 617 Squadron, was a friend. Geoffrey Moir was a Navigation Officer and Second Pilot flying 60 missions. Apart from once flying a Wellington, with bullet holes filled with chewing gum, Geoffrey flew Lancasters. Because they undertook night raids, Geoffrey and his colleagues flew the whole time without fighter support. There were many occasions when they thought things were about to come on top. Consequently the airmen had a reputation for wine, women and song as they thought that before too long they might die. At the end of the war Geoffrey was sent as Security Officer to Croydon Airport through which passed a number of war criminals and traitors. Geoffrey is very proud to have been one of Bomber Harris' boys.

Geoffrey Moir is modest about being awarded a DFC and Bar. When asked how he won these, he laughs and says it was 'for playing silly buggers'!

After demobilisation Geoffrey returned to his former job at the Croydon Gas Company. In the evenings he would give lectures. It was during one of these that he was spotted as a potentially good teacher and encouraged to join the teaching profession, which he did. From 1946 to 1956 Geoffrey taught at Woodside Primary School and in 1956 joined the staff of Ashburton School where he remained for 26 years until his retirement in 1982.

Despite a keen interest in Geography, Geoffrey chose to teach English as he did not want to mix a hobby with work. He gave freely of his time outside school hours. At Woodside Primary School he was involved with the Boxing Club and became an Instructor for the Croydon Amateur Boxing Club. He used to take parties of school pupils up to Pilgrim Fort, a camp on top of Caterham Hill run by Croydon Education Committee. Ashburton School was the first school to use Croydon Education Committee's camp site at Dieppe where Geoffrey and two colleagues set up camp every Easter. Geoffrey also led trips for school pupils to Sweden, across Iceland and across the Sahara in a minibus.

Geoffrey's 'retirement', however, did not last long; within weeks he was flying out to The Falklands to teach there. The islands impressed him greatly and he has written two fascinating books about them.

Still hardly retired, Geoffrey now tours the country giving talks on topics of great interest to him, largely The Falklands, and his treks across Norway, Iceland and the Sahara. He also gives Philatelic Displays. Geoffrey is a Fellow of the Royal Geographical Society. He is a noted after-dinner speaker. It was a privilege to meet this exceptional person.

PROF. CYRIL W. LLOYD

Professor Cyril W. Lloyd (Cy to his friends) is Professor of Composition at the Royal Academy of Music and Head of Music at Fulham Cross High School. Cy has a wide range of teaching experience and remains in touch with many of his former pupils. He receives frequent commissions to write music. Among his many compositions is the Lullaby for Prince William. This was first performed by 100 young musicians at the Royal Academy of Music on 26 February 1983.

GEORGE SHUTTLEWORTH

George's friend and neighbour, Dudley Cary, writes:

George Shuttleworth is a great local character. He is in his 90s and was a Merchant Seaman during World War II. For years George has put out his flags and bunting to celebrate all great occasions. He goes to the Cenotaph and local gatherings in his electric trike. This photo was for D Day 1999 and who should walk round the corner when I was about to take it but XX (local politician) who insisted in being in the picture ('Bloody cheek' said George). Also in the picture is my granddaughter, Marishka Regan, who gets into everything. (D.C.)

OTHER LOCAL HEROES

Mrs Beeton did not actually live in Addiscombe herself but we have included her for two reasons. Her stepfather, Henry Dorling, used to race horses at Woodside Racecourse and from 1869 to 1878 owned Stroud Green House which used to stand on what is now Ashburton Park. The other reason for including Mrs Beeton is that her famous *Book of Household Management* (1861) was aimed at just the kind of ladies who were moving in to the newly-built villas in the Addiscombe area, that is the new middle classes. The book covered every aspect of running a home with recipes and words of practical advice on such topics as how to be a good mistress of a house, managing servants, being a good hostess and good guest, management of children, sick nursing and legal memoranda.

Isabella Mary Beeton was only 22 when she compiled her work which instantly became a best seller and has never been out of print since. Her husband, Samuel Beeton, published *The Englishwoman's Domestic Magazine*; Isabella's *Household Management* was a supplement to this and became so popular it was published separately as her famous book. The recipes were supplied by friends and readers of the magazine and were all tested by either Mrs Beeton herself or her staff. They represent not only traditional British cookery but dishes from all over the world. Although many of the recipes contain familiar ingredients, there are one or two unusual ones: 'Blackbird Pie' and 'Roasted Thrush' to name but two. Sadly Mrs Beeton died of puerperal fever a few days after giving birth to her fourth child at the age of 28.

R.F. Delderfield (1912-1972) lived in Ashburton Avenue from 1918 to 1923. He went on to become a writer of several popular novels. His two books *The Dreaming Suburb* and its sequel *The Avenue Goes to War* are set in Addiscombe and follow the fortunes of various occupants of a road he calls 'The Avenue' (Bingham Road?) from just after the First World War to just after the Second. These two books can currently be borrowed from Ashburton Library. Perhaps Delderfield's most famous novel was *To Serve Them All Our Days* which was serialised on television. In 1971 Delderfield described childhood in Addiscombe in an autobiography *Overture for Beginners*:

One knew and accepted one's place to the last decimal point. Children attending the local 'Colleges' did not mix with those attending elementary schools. One raised one's cap to adult neighbours, washed carefully behind the ears, and learned to speak civilly but rather distantly to shop assistants.

William Makepeace Thackery (1811-62), author of *Vanity Fair* and *Esmond* was born in Calcutta on 11 July 1811. His father died when he was five and his mother remained in India. In 1818 she married Major Carmichael Smyth who returned to England in 1820. At 11 William was sent to Charterhouse and shortly afterwards his stepfather was appointed to Addiscombe College. William appears to have got on well with Smyth and in one of his earliest letters to his mother from school, asks to be told all about Addiscombe and 'the Gentlemen Cadets' and if 'Papa has got a Cock hat that will fit him.' From 1822 to 1824 Thackery spent his holidays at the mansion which was practically his home between the ages of 11 and 13. Major Smyth was very proud of his stepson's abilities and helped prepare him for his career at Cambridge. Vibart records that 'This great writer and noble-hearted gentleman died suddenly on the morning before Christmas Day, 1862'.

D.H. Lawrence, novelist and poet, taught at Davidson High School from 1908 to 1912. He lodged with Mr John W. Jones, the School Attendance Officer, at 12 Colworth Road and later at number 16. His first book *The White Peacock* was published during this time and he began work on *The Trespasser* in his last few months there. Lawrence received good reports while teaching there but did not enjoy it. He wrote to Mr A.W. MacLeod, a friend of his at Davidson, 'I loathe the idea of school more and more. To think of the amount of blood and spirit I sold the Croydon Education committee for £100 a year makes me wild'. Lawrence was often absent because of ill health so the Education Committee curtailed his salary which annoyed him even more. In 1912 he resigned and went to Germany never to teach again.

Davidson school had two famous pupils for a while: Paul Nihill and Paul Russell, better known as Gary Glitter. It closed in July 1982.

Dr Crippen can hardly be described as a hero but there is an interesting Addiscombe connection here. Barbara Broughton's research tells us that it appears that Ethel Neave the 'other woman in the notorious Dr Crippen case' lived at 10 Parkview Road under the name of Smith. Crippen was executed in 1911 for poisoning his wife and the case is famous for the fact that he was the first murderer to be apprehended by the use of a wireless message. The couple was fleeing to Canada aboard the 'Monrose', Ethel disguised in boy's clothing as Crippen's son. In 1916, as Ethel Nelson, she returned to England and worked as a typist, eventually meeting and marrying a Stanley Smith. Electoral rolls showed that the Smiths lived in Parkview Road from 1945 to 1961. Two adult children joined them in 1947. It has to be wondered if she told them of her infamous history!

Gas mask training 4th Queens at Mitcham Road Barracks on 5 April 1938. These gas marks were superseded by a simplified design with the activated charcoal in the chin. (C.A.)

Air Raid Wardens at Woodside School (probably 1943). The Wardens were key to dealing with the raids, working with the police, fire, ambulance and other services to restore normality after each bomb exploded. Ernest Taberner was ARP Controller throughout the war. (C.L.S.L.)

Chapter 14
Second World War

by Tony Stelling

INTRODUCTION

"The only part of the whole scheme is that I don't take your advice."

The author of this chapter refers to Croydon's boundaries as they existed until 1964, when Coulsdon and Purley merged with Croydon.

Several entries in the chapter are from interviews with a number of residents who have memories of the wartime period. They gave a first-hand view, albeit 60 years on, of life in Croydon at that time. My thanks to them all and also to the staff at the Local Studies section at the Central Library. They include Constance Brennan, Celia Young, Norman Holt, Val Grimes, Eddy Munt, Eleanor McDonald, Michael Carpenter, Liz Goodall, Doreen Buckley, Geoff Stelling, Dorothy West, Jim and Pam Davis.

Where I have found a conflict between statistics and dates in these publications, I have chosen the figure that I believe to be the most likely. Undoubtedly there are errors, for which I apologise. This account is necessarily brief and incomplete. Readers wishing to pursue any topic should visit the Local History Archive at the Central Library.

The Second World War came early to Croydon. Situated as it is to the south of London, it was quickly realised that not only would Croydon become a target for bombing, but that the last line of defence for London would be the RAF airfields in Kent and Surrey - especially Croydon, Kenley and nearby Biggin Hill.

In the event hardly any streets escaped from the bombing and about 1000 civilians died as a result. Over 2000 houses were destroyed, and nearly 100 000 houses were damaged to some degree. Evacuation, which started immediately, resulted in the population of Croydon reducing from 240 000 to less than 200 000, although this soon increased as military staff moved into the area. The 1500 allotments at the outbreak of war had increased to 10 000 by 1945. War-damage repairs at the expense of the War Damage Commission totalled £8 million (about £1 billion at today's prices).

Food, clothing and fuel rationing were introduced (and ended long after the hostilities stopped). Identity cards and gas masks had to be carried at all times. Everyone had access to some form of bomb shelter, whether at home or at work, at school or near the shops.

Young men and women joined the armed forces or were directed to other jobs. Factories were converted to the function of war-work. Many children – and their mothers – left Croydon for safer places. Empty houses were requisitioned for war purposes. Hospitals reserved many beds for bombing injuries.

Society changed radically during the war, but the sense of community was never stronger.

THE DOMESTIC SCENE

Life went on, couple's married, babies were born, and people became ill and died. The offices and factories provided work. The trains, buses and trams continued their regular services. The Post Office provided daily deliveries. Children went to school. Lawns still needed mowing. Cooking, cleaning and ironing remained household chores... but alongside all this, the world had changed beyond all recognition. Families were broken up by evacuation and by military or other duties. Men and women in Croydon worked long hours at regular jobs, and then spent their nights on ARP (Air Raid Precautions) or fire watching or Home Guard duties. Everyone going about their daily routines carried the ubiquitous gas mask (issued in mid 1939).

The television network (still in its infancy) was closed, but wireless thrived. Cars were laid up because of petrol restrictions. Gardens were transformed to vegetable plots (often with bomb shelters). The 'blackout' meant that life was difficult after dark. Eleanor remembers that, alighting at East Croydon after a day at the Ministry of Information, she had to take great care to ensure she stepped on to a platform and not on to the lines. She also recollects walking home each evening to Bisenden Road, and worrying whether her house and family had survived the bombing. Michael remembers a Canadian Army lorry crashing over the parapets of the bridge at

135

Gas mask training. (C.L.S.L.)

Thousands of Croydon children were evacuated to safer places.
Does any reader know who these children are? This photograph was taken in Cherry Orchard Road
during the first phase of evacuation in September 1939. (C.A.)

Street Party at Rymer Road and the children are back on home ground, 1945. (B.B.)

Sandilands and tumbling on to the railway tracks below. The accident, in which two died, was blamed on the poor lighting. The wardens kept a close eye on the blackout; each chink of light merited a reprimand. Headlights for vehicles were no more than narrow slits, and there was no street lighting.

There were shortages of everything; food, clothes, fuel, toys, etc. Queuing became a way of life - especially for food. Val recollects that her grandfather grew vegetables in his Clyde Road garden and swapped onions and carrots for cheese with a family further up the road. Norman remembers keeping rabbits in Shirley - but he did not enjoy the resultant pies. Dorothy told me how the firemen at the fire stations spent their spare time between raids repairing and making toys for local children. Liz remembers her mother preserving eggs in isinglass, and salting beans. One cold winter day marmalade made with hard won oranges, and sugar saved from the rations, was to be bottled. Unfortunately the glass jars were too cold - and they all cracked, a minor tragedy.

Croydon was a town with few children in late 1939. Evacuation started on Monday 4 September and by that evening 20 000 children, mothers and teachers had left the town, mainly for Brighton and Hove. Twelve-year-old Norman was on a family holiday in the Isle of Wight, and stayed there for several days before going to join his school (Selhurst Grammar School for Boys) at their temporary location in Hove. Latterly SGSB moved to Bideford whilst the adjacent Girls' Grammar School evacuated to Guildford. All Croydon's council schools closed for six months. During the 'phoney' war many children returned to Croydon and many schools re-opened in April 1940 with small numbers of pupils and teachers. Jim was at Whitgift School during the 1940/41 bombs. He remembers that schoolwork was badly affected by the raids; he frequently had to try to work in the school shelters, which at that time were not much more than covered trenches. (Whitgift did not evacuate.). During the ensuing years evacuation slowed to a trickle. It peaked again during the flying bombs of autumn 1944 when 36 000 children and parents left their homes for safer places in a period of 15 weeks.

Top: Painting the curb white - Rosa Hurn (née Gray) and friend Margery Ashworth (née Warner) in Edward Road on 3 September 1939, the day war was announced. Rosa's parents look on in front of the house in which she was born. The blackout caused many accidents and kerb painting was a valuable safety measure. (R.H.)

Left: Geoff Stelling in 4th Queens uniform with sister, June, in 1940. Later in the war, Geoff, who came from Woodside, became a bomber pilot. (T.S.)

National Registration day was on 29 September 1939. The Town Clerk, Ernest Taberner, administered a complete census, which became the basis for identity cards, and all forms of rationing. On attaining the age of 18 each person became liable for 'call up'. Most young men joined the armed services, whilst the young women had many options - ranging from military service to being a Land Girl on the farms. Constance was directed to work as a driver, and in the following years drove for a greengrocer, a laundry, Oliver Typewriters (Gloucester Road), and finally at Redwing Aircraft in Bensham Lane. Many young people found themselves far from home and family for the first time in their lives. Once again families were split up, often not meeting again for years. Eddy remembers his older brother joining the Army in 1940, and meeting him not far from the appaling conflict at Monte Casino in 1943. They did not meet again until 1948.

As the months went by large numbers of military people moved into Croydon, and many lived with local families. Unoccupied houses were requisitioned for the use of Anti-Aircraft gunnery crews and the like. Many of the large Victorian houses in Radcliffe Road were used in this way. Most of them are no longer there, having been replaced by smaller modern houses in the 1960s.

The first ration books for food were issued in January 1940, and typical weekly rations for an adult were:

Bacon and Ham	4oz (100g)
Meat to value of	1s.2d. (6p)
Butter	2oz (50g)
Cheese	2oz (50g)
sometimes up to 4oz or 8oz	
Margarine	4oz (100g)
Cooking Fat	4oz (100g)
sometimes down to 2oz	
Milk	3 pints
sometimes down to 2 pints	
Plus dried milk	
Sugar	8oz (225g)
Preserves	1lb jar (450g) every 2 months
Tea	2oz (50g)
Eggs	1 fresh
sometimes down to 1 every fortnight	
Plus dried eggs	
Sweets	12oz
(350g) every 4 weeks	

There was also a monthly 'points' system allowing the purchase of other rationed items such as dried fruit or tinned fish and meat.

Croydon Victory
Vegetable Show & Fete
IN AID OF THE
RED CROSS
AGRICULTURE FUND

SCHEDULE OF PRIZES
and
RULES FOR EXHIBITORS
on the following dates and places
1942

August 3rd (Bank Holiday) - Ashburton Park
entries close July 25th
August 15th
Thornton Heath Recreation Ground
entries close August 8th
August 29th · · · · · · Wandle Park
entries close August 22nd

GENERAL SECRETARY,
THE BOROUGH VALUER,
71, PARK LANE,
CROYDON 4435 (Ext. 236).   CROYDON

First Show closes at 7.30 p.m.
Second Show   7.0 p.m.
Third Show   6.30 p.m.

Vegetables and fruit were not rationed, but were price controlled. Preservation of food by bottling, canning, salting and pickling was another household activity. And if there was any waste food, it was put into street bins to be collected for feeding pigs. The Council helped to organise pig, poultry and rabbit clubs - and my father kept ducks at our house in Upper Norwood.

"Third Floor—no buckets, no scrubbing-boards, no kettles, no electric irons . . ."

Cooking during the war was a challenge - but in hindsight the diet was adequate, and 60 years on it is believed that the wartime diet had a lot to commend it. Before the war many town children were undernourished, but with the advent of rationing, and supplements such as concentrated orange juice, cod liver oil and rosehip syrup the children thrived. At school, extra milk and hot midday meals were provided.

Dorothy remembers that when her husband Maurice in the RAF at Stornoway sent home a box of kippers she gave one to each neighbour. (Later in the War Maurice had been in America, Australia and was at the Salerno landings. On 'D' day he was lucky enough to miss being torpedoed because he was in sick bay with a broken nose - caused during a cricket match!).

Shopping was a bore. When there was anything in stock, there was a queue. But mostly the shops were devoid of new goods. Many of the stores (including the dairies and coal merchants) did home-deliveries, mostly by horse-drawn wagons. Geoff remembers the blacksmith at Woodside Green, busy every day shoeing the horses. Everything that could be reused was. Nothing was thrown away. It was the heyday of home sewing, worn sheets were 'top-to-tailed', curtains became skirts. Even the newspapers had their use in the smallest room. It was the ultimate recycling society - and the word was that the Germans were even better at re-use than us (but we did not copy their ersatz coffee made from acorns!).

Many shopping centres had civic restaurants. The first in Croydon opened in March 1941 in Whitehorse Road, and ultimately there were about 20. Two were in Lower Addiscombe Road at No.59, and 278-80 (which had been the Gas Showrooms nearly opposite the Black Horse). Meals in such places were cheap and nourishing (and not included in the rations). Meat and two vegetables could be had for 6d. The market at Surrey Street continued to provide fruit and vegetables in season (but without the pineapples and bananas of earlier years). Pam was in St Ives for the war years, and remembers her father bringing a banana home for her. An American

Many young women volunteered to work in the munitions factories. Without their efforts our armed services would have been short of weapons and materials to fight the war. (I.W.M.)

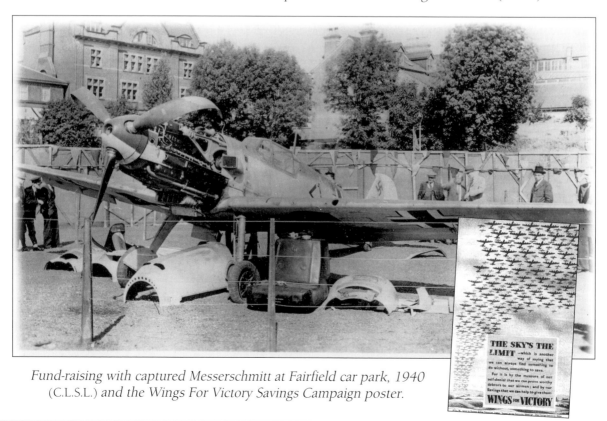

Fund-raising with captured Messerschmitt at Fairfield car park, 1940 (C.L.S.L.) and the Wings For Victory Savings Campaign poster.

airman on an incoming bomber had brought in a bunch. Dorothy had two young children at the start of the war, and remembers that when oranges occasionally appeared, you could get one for each green (children's) ration book. She also recollects Woolton pie (named after the Minister of Food – Lord Woolton). The recipe is given below. The department stores of Kennards, Grants and Allders remained open and survived the worst of the damage. The district shopping centres, such as Lower Addiscombe Road, provided all regular requirements (when they could!).

Woolton Pie

Dice 1lb each of potatoes, cauliflower, swedes and carrots, and cook in salted water.
Strain, but keep ¾ pint of the vegetable water.
Arrange the vegetables in a pie dish.
Add a little vegetable extract and 1oz of rolled oats to the vegetable water and cook until thickened. Pour over the vegetables; add 3-4 chopped spring onions. Top with mashed potatoes, and a very little grated cheese. Heat in the oven until golden brown.
Serve with brown gravy.

Financing the war also affected life at home. Not only was there supplementary taxation (in the form of 'Post War Credits'), but the government also raised funds through National Savings and other campaigns such as 'Warships Week' in 1942 which raised £1.2 million for 'our' destroyer HMS Milne. There were active 'Street' savings groups in each ward administered from the National Savings Shop at 72 George Street.

Croydon's Salvage campaign began in November 1939. By 1945 40 000 tonnes of useful materials, from paper to scrap metals, and from glass to bones, had been collected from the Croydon area raising over £130 000. Each house had its own sack for waste paper. Waste food was collected from canteens for pig swill. Many iron fences and gates had been appropriated for munitions manufacture. If this programme had continued and strengthened, we would perhaps not have experienced the 21st-century problems of dealing with waste by landfill.

Dark evenings at home would be spent listening to the wireless, sewing, knitting or darning, and possibly reading or doing a pre-war jigsaw. Dorothy recollects

"Yes, for the guns: shove 'em down the barrel and shoot 'em out like arrows."

Incident Posts were set up for each Air Raid. This shows Woodville Road in Thornton Heath, after a doodlebug on 3 July 1944. (C.L.S.L.)

cutting up most of Maurice's civilian shirts and trousers to make children's clothes. Children's comics such as Dandy and Beano flourished. I well remember radio programmes like 'Monday Night at Eight', 'Appointment with Fear' and ITMA. 'Saturday Night Theatre' attracted record audiences. The BBC News kept the people informed (and sometimes misinformed) about the war; newspapers were censored, as they had been during the First World War.

Keeping warm was a problem during the cold weather; January 1940 broke records in Croydon with great drifts of snow and 22 degrees of frost. Voluntary rationing of fuel was instituted, becoming compulsory in 1942. An average householder in the later stages of the war could get about three tonnes of coal a year for boiler and grates. There was much advertising to encourage the use of as little gas, electricity and coal as possible.

Social life outside the home was also disrupted. Theatres and cinemas re-opened after briefly closing in September 1939. They provided an essential diversion from the tedium (and the horrors) of daily life in wartime. The Scala, the Davis, the Grand and the Empire are just memories now. A bomb fell on the crowded Davis theatre on 14 January 1944. Luckily

Left: *The simple Anderson shelter in the garden provided considerable protection. This shows the devastation at Spring Park Road, Shirley on 26 July 1944 - with only minor damage to the shelter.* (C.L.S.L.)

Below: *3.7 inch anti-aircraft gun at Hayes, Kent. These guns were strategically sited where they could defend London against the bombers. They were 'air-burst' weapons relying on accurate fusing so that the shells exploded near to the attacking aircraft.* (I.W.M.)

Above: *Clyde Road Nursing Home destroyed by a high explosive bomb that fell near Addiscombe Road Junction on 29 September 1940.* (C.L.S.L.)

Above: *Capri Road after the V1 fell on 1 July 1944 devastating a wide area around Dalmally Road. Strict censorship meant that little detailed information about the bombs was published. 142 V1 Flying Bombs fell in Croydon killing 215 people and destroying over 1000 homes.*

Far left: *Addiscombe's first raid on 5 September 1940 devastated several houses in Brockenhurst Road and damaged all services.* (Both C.L.S.L.)

"I've told that five seconds after the whirring sound stops it shouts a rude remark by Goebbels."

it did not explode, but even so seven people died and many were injured. Had it exploded the death toll would have been terrible. Allders was seriously damaged in the same raid. Children of the 1940s remember Saturday morning cinema (6d.) with affection.

The public libraries were popular despite the reduced opening hours. There were also concerts, dances and socials in local halls, and ballroom dancing thrived. There were many parades and events organised with the aim of trying to involve the civilian population in the 'fighting' war going on in so many places around the world. Sport thrived at amateur levels, and professional sport (soccer, horse racing, etc.) survived – although large assemblies of people were discouraged during the worst of the bombing. There was a crowd of 90 000 at Wembley for the 1945 Southern Cup Final where Chelsea beat Millwall 2-0. The gate money of £29 000 would hardly pay a leading player's weekly wage now!

Public transport by bus, tram and train continued to be the main way of getting about. The heyday of the private car was yet to come, and during the war private motoring was almost impossible because of fuel controls. Croydon Corporation powered many of its vehicles with methane gas extracted from the sewage works (the use of methane saved 85 000 gallons of petrol per year in the later stages of the war). Some buses also used gas carried in trailers. From 1933 there had been plans to replace many trams by trolley buses, but this programme was halted by the war, and indeed trams continued to run until 1951. Bombing disrupted public transport frequently, and travel to and from work was often a problem, especially during the winter of 1940. Celia remembers a journey to Essex in 1941 when the train she was on was bombed and machine gunned. Since the train was immobilised, she continued by bus and appreciated the kindness of the local station master.

In the south of the borough large concrete blocks to impede any invasion forces obstructed some roads. Liz remembers these blocks, and a 'pill-box' being built at the southern end of Park Hill Rise where she was living.

No bombs fell locally until 17 June 1940 at Addington, and on 15 August 1940 the storms of war were unleashed in Croydon with the attack on Croydon Aerodrome. Many remembered the broadcast by Lord Haw Haw on 26 October 1939:

Croydon must beware. She is the second line of defence. We know the aerodrome is camouflaged but we know just what kind of camouflage it is. We shall bomb it and bomb it to a finish, and would advise the people there to evacuate the area this next weekend, as we shall do the job thoroughly. But we shall be merciful and use only incendiary bombs.

Few people took any notice of the broadcast – but I am sure that our gunners were on red alert.

Suddenly the phoney war was over – and air raid sirens became a daily occurrence and from August to December 1940 the sirens sounded 381 times (nearly three times a day). Overhead the Battle of Britain raged above South London, Surrey and Kent. The beauty of the lacy vapour trails belied the death and destruction. Luftwaffe losses were so heavy that Germany switched to night bombing. Croydon residents remember that the fires in East London and the Docks were sometimes so bright that it was possible to read a newspaper in the garden at night. Householders who had not already put up shelters, or reinforced basements, rushed to do so. Standardised domestic shelters came in two varieties. Firstly, in 1940 the Anderson shelter which was an arched corrugated iron structure sunk about 2'6" into the ground and covered with a thick layer of soil. It had a rear emergency exit and could accommodate up to four people. By 1941 about 30 000 had been installed in Croydon but many became waterlogged and had to be concreted. Whilst some had heat and light, most were damp and cheerless places – not an attractive option to staying warm in bed!

The second was the Morrison shelter introduced in 1941. This was a table-like structure on the ground floor with very cramped accommodation. It was strong enough to hold the weight of a house collapsing on top. These were still being installed in 1944 during the V1 bombing at a cost of £7 each. They were free to lower wage earners. During the bombing Eleanor's family squeezed under the stairs. They thought the risks of pneumonia in an outside shelter were greater than the bombs. She remembers an incendiary device, which set alight the ivy climbing up the fence. After using her bucket of sand to no avail, she borrowed a neighbour's sand. This put the fire out. Next day she got a bill from the neighbour for 9d. to replace the sand! By 1944 there was a certain fatalistic attitude towards the bombs, especially the V1s (nicknamed Doodlebugs). They came day and night, and if you heard the motor cut out it was too late to shelter. A few seconds later the bang, and once again someone else had copped it! Croydonians adapted to the irritations of the sirens sounding at inconvenient moments.

Some places which had been attacked during the First World War, were bombed again in the Second. Liz's grandfather Dr Thomson lived at 'Glendalough' at the junction of Morland Road and Lower Addiscombe Road. In October 1915 a Zeppelin bombed it causing extensive damage. No one was injured. (This site – now a Co-op store – was extensively damaged in the 1941 bombing.).

Being bombed out was an awful experience even if there were no deaths or injuries. The family had to find other accommodation with neighbours or in the Council Rest Homes. Furniture and contents had to be stored for return to the owners at a later date. The house had to be made secure or knocked down. About 2000 families were indeed 'bombed out', some several times.

Val remembers the large bomb which destroyed the Nursing Home at 159 Addiscombe Road at the south end of Clyde Road (now 'Beverley Hyrst'). It took the roof off her grandfather's house (No.81 now renumbered as 22) rendering it uninhabitable. When the house contents were recovered later, she recollects the jars of strawberry jam – which had crystallised. They were delicious. Liz told me that after this bomb, a large site was cleared at the end of Clyde Road and American troops helped to install some prefabs as temporary housing for bombed-out families. Constance remembers the bomb that annihilated No.28 Addiscombe Road (now an office block). The owner Mr Egleton was an Air Raid Warden who was outside at the time. His false teeth were blown out – and never recovered. After bomb damage had been assessed, immediate (first-aid) repairs were carried out, to allow the house to be used. Later in the war, Italian prisoners of war were employed to help with bomb damage repairs. These Italian POWs were housed in camps nearby, but there is a dearth of information on this subject.

In many households one or more of the family were away with the armed forces or on other duties, and others were evacuated. For most people letters were the only means of communication, and most of these were censored. At the outbreak of war postal deliveries were reduced from 4 to 3 each day and collections from 10 to 6. Urgent communications was often by telegram (few people had telephones). A telegram from the War Office could often bring bad news of death or injury to loved ones. Over 2000 service men and women of Croydon died between 1939 and 1945. They are remembered in memorials at the Town Hall and elsewhere. (The Croydon section of the 'National Inventory of War Memorials' is available at Croydon Local Studies Library.).

It was ten years or more before home life showed signs of recovery from the war. The scars healed, but the world would never return to how it was in 1939. A monster had been slain, but we would never regain the innocence of earlier times.

CROYDON AT WAR

It is impossible 60 years on to understand the complexity of relationships involved in Croydon's war – the Government departments and the local councils; the regular forces and the Home Guard; the Police, the hospitals, the ambulance service, the ARP, the fire service and so on. In addition most of the freedoms we recognise in peacetime were put in abeyance. You could be conscripted into the Army, or directed into a job. Your children were evacuated. Your food was rationed and the prices controlled. Moving house was regulated, and anyway there was no new house building.

Yet it was a popular war. Coming as it did after the years of depression there was suddenly a sense of purpose and spirit, and, not least, there was full employment – indeed many people worked 12-hour shifts and then did fire watching or Home Guard duties for several evenings a week. Eddy's day job in 1941 was at 'Harper's Automatic Machines' (a market leader in coin-operated vending machines) in Stafford Road which had changed to accommodate war work. The factory was a 24-hour operation making munitions. The bomb casings Eddy worked on were for hanging under the wings of Hurricanes, and they had to be machined very accurately. The women in the factory were making fuses and detonators, etc. Celia did an office job by day, but in the evenings/nights she was on ambulance duties twice a week. It is interesting to note that in 1939 there were only four regular ambulances based at the fire stations. The wartime ambulance service initially had six ambulances (later I estimate 20 including cars for sitting casualties) staffed around the clock by women (480 in 1940, falling to 160 in 1944).

Bombs were the principal problem! Croydon was lucky enough to avoid the saturation of bombing seen elsewhere. However, the RAF aerodromes at Croydon and Kenley were targets, and so were the railways. The Addiscombe area was largely residential and had few factories worth targeting; Creed's headquarters teleprinter/telegraphy factory at the corner of Cherry Orchard Road (now Knolly's House) escaped damage, but Gowllands Optical Works in Morland Road was hit several times.

However, we were on the route of the Luftwaffe bombers heading for London from Northern France. This meant that we had to have very active Anti-Aircraft defenses with guns, searchlights, and barrage balloons.

Geoff had joined the 'Queen's' (4th Battalion The Queen's Royal West Surrey Regiment) in 1938 (aged 18) whilst working for Surridge Dawson (Newspaper Distribution). The Queen's was an Anti-Aircraft Searchlight

"How would you like your egg this month, dear?"

Battalion, based at Mitcham Road Barracks, and was a Territorial Army unit. Called up in August 1939, he spent the next 18 months on Anti-Aircraft duties, until he volunteered for flying training with the RAF. He told me that he was 'fed up with being on the wrong end of the beam being shot at, and wanted an opportunity to attack the enemy'. Meanwhile his parent's house in Woodside had been requisitioned for Canadian troops. After training (mainly in South Africa) he spent the last two years of the war flying Wellington torpedo bombers in the Mediterranean searching for, and attacking, enemy shipping.

Croydon also needed effective local services to deal with the death and destruction delivered from the sky. The ARP Act (1937) established the responsibility of local councils to provide a secure infrastructure for dealing with the effects of air raids. Berwick Sayers writes that the East ARP headquarters was at 192 Addiscombe Road; however, I believe that it was at Bernhard House 192 Lower Addiscombe Road (a large Victorian house near Bingham Corner). There was a small public bomb shelter, for 21 persons, in a basement at 94 Addiscombe Road (near Sandilands). There were many other public shelters, and factories, offices, schools and hospitals all had their own. Many were no more than covered trenches in the first months of the war.

When a bomb fell the damage varied from a hole in the garden to the complete devastation of several houses. And sometimes the bomb did not explode at all – which meant that men had to put their lives at risk to disarm it. The most destructive bombs were those that exploded at ground level without a deep crater – the parachute land mines and the V1 flying bombs of 1944 were like this. In general the isolated incendiary was not much of a problem. The local AA guns (emplacements on Lloyd Park with searchlights) supported the RAF fighters in attacking the bombers – but these guns themselves caused blast damage, and a few unexploded AA shells landed in the south of the borough.

Michael's father was in the Home Guard manning some of the guns at the North end of Mapledale Avenue. There were eight 3.7 inch guns, a Bofors and a Lewis machine gun. Later in the war these were directed by electric servo-motors and could deliver more fire power. On the first night of the V1s one gun fired 750 shells; initially the gunners were delighted that they were 'hitting' the pilotless aircraft because of the flame from the back. Next morning they were informed that this was the start of Hitler's new 'secret weapon'. They hadn't hit any. Subsequently the AA guns and the fighters had considerable success in preventing the V1s reaching London. The Royal Observer Corps had a post at Creed's factory, and provided continuous reporting of raids in progress.

Quite often in the early part of the war German planes machine gunned people in the streets. Eddy's wife was machine gunned twice, and bombed out three times. Michael's (nine years old) most exciting incident was when he heard the sound of machine guns near Addiscombe Road whilst on his way to school by bike. He took cover behind a wall. Doreen's father was caught in the same incident when he was shopping (for eggs) in Lower Addiscombe Road.

There is an apocryphal story that the German pilot responsible for killing some schoolchildren on that day was caught by Polish aircrew when his plane crashed near Biggin Hill RAF fighter station. It is said that they threw him into his burning aeroplane.

Eddy remembers many bombs first hand including the spectacular explosion on 10 October 1940 when the largest Gas Holder was hit. On Sunday evening, 24 November 1940, the Town Hall was badly damaged, and the Working Man's Club in Scarbrook Road received a direct hit. Eddy (16 years of age) had been on sentry duty guarding the enormous water pumps behind Surrey Street. He recalls 'that's where I first saw my lowest form of British people, where they were robbing the pennies from the pinboard machines instead of trying to save the lives of the people who needed rescuing.' A few weeks earlier, on 28 October, he was in the large public bomb shelter in the basement of the newly opened 'Electric House' in Wellesley Road where 600 people were sheltering. During the raid a large bomb entered through the bronze doors and exploded in the shelter killing 10 and injuring nearly 100.

He also recollects training with the AA guns in Lloyd Park near Sandilands, so that he could stand in for the regular gunners at night when they had a few days' break. He says 'I used to thoroughly enjoy that, it was really up my street!' Much later in the war, Norman, by then a student apprentice with the Electricity Undertaking, was on duty on the evening of Sunday 30 July 1944 when a V1 did severe damage. He remembers:

Its wing clipped a cooling tower and then it descended into the turbine hall of the power station, blew the roof off and did no small damage to one of the big turbo-alternators which had the casing removed for repairs.

Ministry of Works staff arrived next morning and within 48 hours power was back on line.

Addiscombe, Shirley and nearby areas suffered severely. The air-raid warning sounded first within an hour of the declaration of war on 3 September 1939 (a false alarm). From 1940 the records show the alarm was sounded many times: 1940: 381 times, 1941: 138 times, 1942: 22 times, 1943: 108 times, 1944: 510 times, 1945: 14 times.

THE GERMAN WAY

Cartoon from Punch, *May 1940.*

There were 142 V1s (more than in any other London borough). The last bomb of the war to fall on Croydon was a V2 rocket on 26 January 1945 (in Lloyd Park). Michael believes that this is the one that killed two ATS gunners at the AA emplacement. He had been tobogganing with a school friend and was on his way home in the dusk when the explosion occurred.

It would be invidious to attempt to say which of the bombs was worse than another. The bomb that killed your parents or your child or destroyed your house was the worst one for you. The Borough Engineer's report on air-raid damage records most incidents in some detail and I have listed most of the local incidents at the end of this chapter.

By 1943 it was evident that an invasion from Germany was extremely unlikely, and in 1944 the Home Guard was stood down. The final parade was on 26 November 1944. Whilst it had never had to withstand an invasion, it had been a key member of teams involved in dealing with casualties and air-raid damage. In later days the

Home Guard served at Anti-Aircraft gun emplacements, freeing regular soldiers for other duties.

VE (Victory in Europe) day was on 8 May 1945. Croydon rejoiced, and the street parties went on into the small hours. Four months later VJ (Victory over Japan) day came with more muted celebrations.

Now, in 2000, the bomb sites and the Static Water tanks have all gone. The craters in Lloyd Park may still contain debris, but even they have merged into the landscape we all know well. Occasionally unexploded bombs and shells are found when building and excavation work takes place; the Royal Engineers still bravely deal with these incidents.

Above: *A street party Woodside to celebrate the end of the war.* (A.Bo.)
Below: *Street Party at Clyde Hall, VJ Day, 22 September 1945.* (B.B.)

REFERENCES:
Sayers, B., *Croydon and The Second World War* (1949)
Boast, C.E., *The Borough Engineer's Report on Air Raid damage 1940-44*
Other books too numerous to mention, including *Wards Directories, Croydon Courageous, Courageous Croydon, Croydon in the 1940s and 1950s, We'll Eat Again* and *The Avenue goes to War* (R.F. Delderfield).

Extracts from 'The Borough Engineer's Report on Air Raid Damage 1940-1944' by Mr C.E.Boast (Collated by Tony Stelling, July 2000)

Bombings of Addiscombe, Woodside and Park Hill (not including bombed fields, parks & Golf Courses.

Key: *HE = High Explosive (various types), land mine or parachute mine. Large explosive effect, sometimes 'delayed action'; IB = Incendiary - Magnesium or Phosphorus - often dropped in clusters; OIL = Oil bomb - canister of crude oil plus ignition device; FLY = V1 (Pilotless aircraft) often referred to as a Doodlebug. Powered by a pulse jet engine; V2 = A rocket with a large warhead. The last of Hitler's secret weapons.*

Date	Location	Bomb	Damage and Comments
5/9/40	Ashburton Avenue	1	Nos. 22 and 24 wrecked.
5/9/40	Bingham Road	1	Medium crater damaging sewer (surface water).
5/9/40	Brockenhurst Road	2	No. 16 wrecked, 14 and 18 badly damaged. Foul and surface water sewers damaged. Gas, Water and Electricity mains damaged. (Crater in road) Rear part of Catholic Church Hall wrecked.
5/9/40	Elmers Road	?	Shop and 2 houses badly shaken with roof and chimney damage. Peculiar. May have been due to gas explosion.
5/9/40	Elmgrove Road	2	Nos. 32, 34, 16 wrecked; Nos. 30, 14, 18 badly damaged.
5/9/40	Pagehurst Road	1	Back brick wall in garden of 341 Lower Addiscombe Rd. demolished. Crater in road; damage to Post Office & Gas
5/9/40	Tenterden Road	1	No. 14 wrecked; Nos. 10, 12, 16 badly damaged.
5/9/40	Wydehurst Road	1	Crater on road. Sewers, water and gas mains damaged.
8/9/40	Lower Addiscombe Rd	1 or 2	One very large bomb (or two bombs fastened together) caused very great havoc when it fell at the junction of Lower Addiscombe Road and Parkview Road. 3 houses were wrecked; 1 damaged beyond repair and 3 very badly damaged. Substantial other damage to nearby shops and houses. This crater is the biggest yet seen in Croydon and measures 55ft across the banked earth. All mains supplies and sewers broken.
13/9/40	Fitzjames/Upfield Jcn	1	Crater in road junction. Foul and surface water sewers and water main.
13/9/40	Fitzjames Avenue	1	Nos. 57, 59 cracked and damaged.
13/9/40	Fitzjames Avenue	1	No. 63 back garden. Not much damage.
13/9/40	Fitzjames Avenue	1	Behind No. 65 almost touching house. Very bad cracking
13/9/40	Fitzjames Avenue	AA shell	No. 40 - very little damage.
13/9/40	Upfield	1	Partly demolishing rear and badly cracking No. 3. Damage to outhouses No. 5.
13/9/40	Upfield	OIL	Not much damage.
15/9/40	Altyre Road	1	Behind No. 4, wrecking rear of house.
15/9/40	Bingham Road	1 (large)	No. 142 unstable. Sides out at No. 134. Nos. 136, 138, 140 wrecked. Very serious damage to houses from "Ashdown" (side of Sherwood Road) to No. 135 (side of Kingscote Road).
15/9/40	Bingham Road	1 (heavy)	Crater behind No. 60. Nos. 58, 60 unstable.
15/9/40	Canning Road	1	Behind No.48; Wrecked No.48 kitchen, damaged No. 47 kitchen.
15/9/40	Clyde Road	1	In front of Nos. 78 and 79. Front of 78 out. No. 79 damaged
15/9/40	Colin's Garage near PO sorting office	1	UNEXPLODED - has been sandbagged.
15/9/40	Lower Addiscombe Rd	1	Turner's Garage - repair shop wrecked.
15/9/40	Morland Avenue	1	No. 21 demolished; No. 19 partially wrecked; No. 23 damaged.
15/9/40	Warren Road	1	Behind No. 3; Nos. 2, 5, 8, 9, 10 slight damage. Kendall Court flats damaged.
19/9/40	Sefton Road	1	In road in front of No. 49; Moderate damage to roofs and windows at 45 to 51. Gas main damaged.
21/9/40	Fitzjames Avenue	1	Behind No. 5; Roofs and windows of Nos. 5 and 7 seriously damaged. Roofs and windows in Fitzjames, Sandilands and Addiscombe Road damaged.

SECOND WORLD WAR

Date	Location	Bomb	Damage and Comments
21/9/40	Sandilands	1	Behind No. 16; Nos. 12, 14, 16 and 18 damaged, and in a lesser degree other roofs and windows. In these last two incidents it was particularly noticeable that the bombs had an extra-ordinarily severe blast effect. Pieces of the bomb showed that it had a very thick casing.
27/9/40	Fryston Avenue	OIL	Comparatively little damage.
27/9/40	**No 2** L. Add. Rd	1 very heavy 500lb	Nos. 321, 323, 325, 327 wrecked (chemist, laundry, antique shop, snack bar). Nos. 319, 329 badly damaged (Hairdresser, Paper shop). No. 331 and surrounding properties - lesser damage. No casualties.
27/9/40	Sefton Road	Oil	Between Nos. 27 and 29. Slight fire. Little damage.
28/9/40	Leslie Grove	1	Nos. 18 and 20 wrecked. Nos. 16 and 22 partially demolished, and others considerably damaged. Nos. 1-29, 2-14 and 24-30 badly damaged
28/9/40	**No 5** Park Hill Rec.	Parachute mine	Widespread damage roofs, windows, doors etc., particularly in Chatsworth, Barclay, Fairfield, Hazledean, Stanhope Roads and Addiscombe Grove. Damage to shop windows, and other glass as far as West Croydon and the Swan and Sugarloaf.
29/9/40	**No 4** Chepstow Rd	1 very heavy/	Large crater in garden of No. 8 which was demolished. No. 6 wrecked. Damage to windows and roofs of adjoining 2 joined properties.
1/10/40	Addiscombe Road	1	Large crater in back garden of No. 14. Very little damage.
1/10/40	Alpha Road	1	Small crater in front of Nos. 16a and 16b. No serious damage.
1/10/40	Alpha Road	1	Small crater in passage at side of No. 16. Very little damage, apart from glass in Nos. 16 and 18.
1/10/40	Altyre Road junction Hazeldean Road	1	No. 1 Hazeldean Road half demolished. Crater on path and carriageway. Damage to surrounding property. Walls cracked and windows broken in No. 14. Damage to properties in Hazeldean Road. Gas & Water mains damaged.
1/10/40	Cherry Orchard Road	1	Extensive roof damage to delivery van shed of United Dairies. Glass and tiles of buildings broken. Shop windows in the New Parade broken.
1/10/40	Leslie Grove	1	Small crater in back garden of No. 29, which was seriously damaged. Damage to Nos. 31 and 33.
1/10/40	Leslie Grove	1	Crater in back garden of No. 6. Direct Hit on Anderson shelter. Some casualties. Very little additional damage since raid 28th September.
3/10/40	Dickensons Lane Woodside Brickworks	4 inc 2DA	Slight damage to Nos. 610-622 Davidson Road, from railway bridge to No. 165 Tennison Rd., including 5 shops & Nos. 110-148, and Nos. 72-156 Birchanger Road
4/10/40	Amberley Grove	1	Small crater at end of back garden of No. 5. Slight damage to all houses in road & in Morland Road.
4/10/40	Beckford Road	1	Large crater at back of Nos. 37, 39 & 41. All badly damaged. Very little other damage.
4/10/40	Coombe Cliff	OIL	No material damage. Fell in fish pond.
4/10/40	Dickensons Lane	1	Woodside Brickworks - direct hit on kiln. Not very severe damage.
4/10/40	Northway Road	1	Large crater at back of Nos. 61 & 63. No. 65 demolished. 59 & 67 unstable.
8/10/40	Elm Grove Road junct. with Brockenhurst Rd.	2 joined	Nos. 24-30 (inc) demolished. Nos. 9, 18, 20, 22 unstable. Slight damage to Nos. 1 to 7. Windows of all houses in Brockenhurst Road left intact from previous raid now

Date	Location	Bomb	Damage and Comments
			damaged. No. 39 Brockenhurst Road demolished. Nos. 33, 35, 37 badly damaged. Slight damage to Nos. 26 to 50. Remarks; Nos. 32 and 34 demolished in previous raid. All services damaged. This is the largest crater yet made in Croydon (75ft across, 13 feet deep).
9/10/40	Ashburton Park	2xHE	Although only moderate size bombs, the combined blast caused window and roof damage over a wide area, including the library buildings and houses in Lower Addiscombe Road and Spring Lane fronting onto the park.
11/10/40	Lloyd Park	1	Near No. 44 Lloyd Park Avenue. No damage.
13/10/40	Alderton Road	HE	No. 69 wrecked. Back of No. 71 unstable. Slight damage to No. 67.
13/10/40	Beckford Road	HE	Bomb entered back garden of No. 44 Westbourne Road and exploded under ground pushing up footpath in Beckford Road and damaging sewer. Slight roof damage to Nos. 40 & 42 Beckford Road, and Nos. 42 & 44 Westbourne Road.
13/10/40	Meadvale Road	HE	Crater on path and carriageway opposite No. 64. This house badly damaged. Slight roof damage to Nos. 62, 66 & 68.
13/10/40	Meadvale Road	HE	Crater in back garden of No. 49. Demolished about 75 ft of Woodside Brickworks boundary.
13/10/40	Rees Gardens	HE	Nos. 26 & 28 demolished. No. 30 wrecked, No. 32 unstable. Nos. 22 & 24 badly damaged. Window and roof damage to Nos. 14 to 24, 50 to 82 and 77 to 87. Also Nos. 33 to 39 Westbourne Road.
13/10/40	Selhurst Station	2xHE	Cleaning Sheds. 2 craters very close together inside shed. Several coaches wrecked and tracks damaged. Asbestos and glazed roof damaged over a wide area.
16/10/40	Oaks Road	2xHE	Craters in undergrowth of Addington Hills. Telegraph wires down.
16/10/40	Oaks Road (Coombe Farm)	HE	Crater on piggery, pigsty wrecked, 6 pigs killed.
17/10/40	Oaks Road	HE	Crater in woods at Addington Hills about 100 yds south of Furzefield Cottages. Windows of these cottages damaged. Severe blast damage to trees.
17/10/40	Oaks Road	HE	In piggery about 100 yds North-west of above cottages. No damage.
18/10/40	Elgin Road	1	Crater in back garden of No. 9. Slight window damage to Nos. 7, 9, 11, 13, 15. Very little other damage.
18/10/40	Fitzjames Avenue	1	Crater in carriageway opposite No. 9. No damage.
18/10/40	Tunstall Road	1	In yard of Tunstall Optical Company. Slight damage to this factory and adjoining house No. 3.
18/10/40	Woodbury Close	1	In front garden of No. 11. Very slight damage to No. 11.
21/10/40	Grimwade Avenue	HE	On footpath between Nos. 17 and 19. Very slight roof damage.
21/10/40	Sandilands	HE	Behind No. 38. Only damage – Swimming pool destroyed.
25/10/40	Birch Tree Way	HE	V. Heavy. Very large bomb. Nos. 3 & 5 demolished, 1 & 7 wrecked. Severe window and roof damage to Nos. 2 to 20, and 9 to 17. All houses in Ashurst Walk suffered damage. Nos. 321 to 335 and 156 to 166 Addiscombe Road slightly damaged.
25/10/40	Coombe Road	HE	V. Heavy. Large crater wrecking most of 'Pitt Place' and blocking Coombe Road. Nos. 157-163 severely damaged. Window and roof damage to 153, 155 & 165 to 175. Slight

Date	Location	Bomb	Damage and Comments
			window damage to a few houses in Witherby Close.
27/10/40	Mapledale Avenue	HE	Behind No. 27 in garden. No damage.
28/10/40	Addiscombe Road	HE	Large crater in garden behind No. 50. Garage of No. 48 seriously damaged. Window damage to Nos. 46 to 56.
29/10/40	Fitzjames Avenue	HE	Crater in Tennis court behind No. 38. Window and roof damage to Nos. 34 to 48 and 35 to 51, also 7 to 15 Mapledale Avenue and 34 to 44 Upfield, and a few houses in Addiscombe Road between Mapledale Ave. and Upfield.
29/10/40	Fitzjames Avenue	HE	Crater at end of garden behind No. 21. Window and roof damage to Nos. 13 to 29, 6, 12, 14 Fitzjames Avenue; 24 to 28 Addiscombe Road; and Nos. 2, 4 and 6 Mapledale Avenue.
1/11/40	Mapledale Avenue	HE	In garden at rear of No. 23. Window and roof damage to Nos. 19 to 29 and 22 to 26. Nos. 38 to 42 and 45 to 49 and 53 Upfield also damaged.
1/11/40	Radcliffe Road	2xHE	Two large craters close together, one completely blocking the carriageway. Slight window damage to a new house called 'Warwick House' and No. 33.
7/11/40	Ashburton Road	HE	Large crater behind No. 16. Back of house very badly damaged, remainder of house severely shaken. Window and roof damage to Nos. 14, 18, 20 and 22. Window damage only to Nos. 15 to 27, also a few in Northampton Road.
7/11/40	Sefton Road	HE	Large crater in carriageway. No. 35 unstable, Nos. 33 and 37 severely damaged. Window and roof damage to Nos. 20 to 28, 29, 31, 39 and 41. Window damage to Nos. 18, 30 to 36, 21 to 27, and 43 to 49. This area suffered in a previous raid. Gas, Water mains and sewer damaged.
8/11/40	**No 6** Ashling Road	HE	Lloyds Bank and back of No. 210 Lower Addiscombe Road wrecked. No. 214 badly damaged, also No. 2 Ashling Road. All houses in Ashling Road and Claremont Road suffered severe window and roof damage. Shops and houses on both sides of Lower Addiscombe Road from Bingham Road to Teevan Road damaged. Window and roof damage to Nos. 251 to 263 and 204 to 216. Severe window damage to most houses in Colworth Road and a few houses in Bingham Road.
8/11/40	Sonning Road	HE	Nos. 2 to 18 demolished, Nos. 1, 3 & 5 unstable, No. 20 badly damaged, also Nos. 1, 2 & 4 Malcolm Road. Window and roof damage to Messrs Scott & Sons, Timber merchants and most houses in Malcolm Road and Anthony Road. Road completely blocked and all services damaged.
29/11/40	Grimwade Avenue	HE	On vacant land opposite No. 5. Surrounding roofs damaged by blast.
29/11/40	Harland Avenue	HE	In front garden of No. 6. Only slight damage.
29/11/40	Mapledale Avenue	HE	In front garden of 'The Homestead'. No damage
8/12/40	Grimwade Avenue	2xHE	2 craters in open ground between Nos. 2 and 10. No damage.
8/12/40	Grimwade Avenue	HE	Back of No. 9 partially wrecked and rendered unstable, remainder of house and No. 7 badly damaged. Window and roof damage to Nos. 1 to 5, 11, 2, 10 and 12.
8/3/41	**No 8** Bingham Road	HE	Crater in front garden of No. 76. This house and No. 74 badly damaged. Slight window and roof damage to Nos. 72, 78 to 86, 77, 79 and Addiscombe Hall, also a few houses in Parkview Road. This area suffered damage in previous raids.

Date	Location	Bomb	Damage and Comments
8/3/41	Blackhorse Lane	HE	Nos. 38 and 40 demolished, Nos. 36 and 42 unstable. Window and roof damage to Nos. 26 to 34 and 44 to 50. Slight damage to some houses in Woodside Court Road. All services damaged.
8/3/41	Dalmally Road	HE	Crater in back garden of No. 82. Backs of Nos. 78 to 88 badly damaged. Roof damage to Gowllands Factory, Morland Road and window damage to Nos. 46 to 134 and 1 to 83 Dalmally Road.
8/3/41	Elmers Road HE		Nos. 31 and 33 demolished, No. 35 wrecked, Nos. 29 and 37 unstable, Nos. 30 to 40, 25 and 27 badly damaged. Window and roof damage to all other houses in this road, also some windows in Morland Road School.
8/3/41	Southern Railway between Tenterden Rd. and Elmers Rd.	3xHE	1. Crater on embankment. Lock-up garages at Pines School wrecked. 2. On embankment. No damage. 3. Slight damage to down track, and window damage to backs of Nos. 1 to 39 Elmers Road.
8/3/41	Tenterden Road	HE	Crater in Hard Tennis Court. Roof damage to The Pines School. Slight damage to Nos. 5 to 19 Sissinghurst Road.
8/3/41	Tenterden Road	HE	In back garden of No. 1. This house and No. 3 unstable. Slight damage to Nos. 5 to 13.
8/3/41	Woodside Green	HE	Crater in centre of carriageway opposite No. 43. Shops Nos. 39 to 45, 54 and 56 badly damaged. Window and Roof damage to "Joiners Arms" P.H. and shops Nos. 58, 60 and 62. Window damage to all shops from No. 15 to Dickensons Place, including "the Beehive" P.H. and houses 34 to 46. All services damaged. This area suffered in a previous raid.
8/3/41	Woodside Green	HE	Exploded below ground in passage to Adult School. No. 46 very badly cracked, also back of "Joiners Arms" P.H.
16/4/41	Addiscombe Road	HE	Large crater in carriageway opposite Nos. 26 to 28. Front of these houses unstable. Window and roof damage to 35 to 43 , 30 to 38, 22 and 24. Slight window damage to Creeds factory. All services damaged
16/4/41	Baring Road	HE	Nos. 28 to 36 demolished, 38 wrecked and 33 to 39, 26 and 40 unstable. Nos. 31, 41, 22 and 24 badly damaged. Window and roof damage to all remaining houses in this road, all houses in Claremont Road (No. 23 severe), Bingham Road from Claremont Road to Park View Road including St. Mildred's church, also some window damage in Ashling Road, Park View Road and Lower Addiscombe Road. This area suffered in a previous raid.
16/4/41	No 7 Capri Road	HE	Nos. 91 to 97 demolished, 89 and 99 practically wrecked. Window and roof damage to 69 to 87, 101 to 105, and 70 to 112, also in Dalmally Road Nos. 137 to 159 and 170 to 198. Slight window damage to majority of houses in Grant Road.
16/4/41	Chichester Road	HE	Crater in carriageway opposite No. 11. Window damage to 11, 13, 14 and 16. All services damaged.
16/4/41	Elgin Road	HE	Nos. 54 and 56 wrecked, 52 unstable. Window and roof damage to 40 to 50, 58 to 70 and 37 to 87.
16/4/41	Havelock Road	HE	Crater in carriageway. Window and roof damage to 14, 15, 16, 17, 18, 18A and 19. All services damaged.
18/4/41	Elgin Road	HE	In garden at rear of No. 10. This house and Nos. 6, 8 Elgin Road also 1 to 5 Havelock Road received very serious blast damage. Extensive window and roof damage over a radius

Date	Location	Bomb	Damage and Comments
			of 300 yds. This area has suffered severely in previous raids.
18/4/41	Park Hill Road	HE	Small crater on footpath and carriageway between Nos. 34 and 36. Severe blast damage to houses over a radius of 200 yds.
19/4/41	Addiscombe Court Rd	HE	Exploded just above ground behind No. 126, and made no crater. This house wrecked at back, Nos. 124 and 128 unstable. Nos. 118, 120, 122 and 130 very badly damaged. Window and roof damage to Nos. 94 to 116 and 105 to 149. The combined blast from this bomb and the one at Lr. Addiscombe Road rendered Nos. 1, 2, 3 and 4 Leslie Park Road unstable, and did extensive window and roof damage to the Co-operative Dairy. Nos. 2, 4 and 6 Tunstall Road badly damaged. Nos. 8 to 60, 1 to 71, also T.O.C. Factory received window and roof damage, also many houses in Leslie Park Road and Lebanon Road.
19/4/41	Coombe Road	HE	Large crater in garden at rear of 'The Warren', only slight roof damage to adjoining property.
19/4/41	Coombe Road	HE	Crater in field near junction with Melville Avenue. No damage.
19/4/41	No 1 Lower Addiscombe Rd	HE	Crater in carriageway. Nos. 73 to 83 (shops) demolished. Turner's Garage partly wrecked, remainder very badly damaged. No. 100 severely damaged. Window and roof damage to shops and flats over Nos. 85 to 121 and 64 to 80, houses Nos. 63 to 71 and 82 to 96. Window damage to Nos. 123 to 147 including Addiscombe Station, 102 to 130 including Barclay's Bank, and Addiscombe Methodist Church, all houses in Warren Road, some houses in Hastings Road, Morland Road, also several shop windows in Cherry Orchard Road. All services damaged. Mr Frederick Lover aged 32 (Grocer of No. 75) died as a result of injuries. His wife and child escaped unhurt.
10/5/41	Addiscombe Road	HE	Crater in garden of No. 58. No damage.
10/5/41	Canning Road	HE	In garden at rear of No. 10. Slight window damage to Nos. 115 and 117 Tunstall Road
10/5/41	Canning Road	HE	Crater in Tennis Court behind St. Mary Magdalene's Church. No damage
10/5/41	Canning Road	HE	No. 5 practically wrecked. Slight damage to adjoining property. No other damage.
10/5/41	Tunstall Road	HE	Crater in garden at rear of No. 97. Slight window damage to this and adjoining houses. This area suffered in a previous raid.
10/5/41	Tunstall Road	HE	Small temporary workshop wrecked. No other damage.
?/?/43	Lower Addiscombe Rd	HE	Crater in carriageway opposite No. 67. Only slight roof damage to this house by flying debris. All services damaged.
5/11/43	Clyde road	HE	HighBlast. Medium size crater in back garden about 60 ft from No. 159 Addiscombe Road (Nursing Home). This house partially wrecked, also No. 84 Clyde Road. No. 161 Addiscombe Road and Nos. 82 & 83 Clyde Road probably unstable. Blast damage to windows and roofs was very severe and widespread, extending over a radius of 500 yds.
5/11/43	Harland Avenue	HE	In front garden of No. 6. Severe blast damage to front of this house. Minor window and roof damage to Nos. 1 to 13, 2, 4 and 10.

Date	Location	Bomb	Damage and Comments
5/11/43	Sandilands	HE	In garden at rear of No. 41. Severe blast damage to rear of this house and No. 39. Minor window and roof damage to Nos. 35, 37, 32 to 44 Sandilands, and Nos. 32, 34, 36, 35 and 37 Grimwade.
23/2/44	Addiscombe Ward	IBs	Incendiary Bombs scattered over the area Lower Addiscombe Rd, Canning, Tunstall, Addiscombe Court Rd., Lebanon, Leslie Park Road causing rather extensive fire damage at Turners Garage and some houses in the above roads. During this raid seven 50K phosphorus bombs failed to explode in Morland Road and Canning Rd.
24/3/44	Addiscombe Road	IB	No. 343 Upper part burned out.
24/3/44	Bingham Road	IB	No. 6 Upper part burned out.
16/6/44	Brownlow Road Tennants Nursery	FLY	In open Ground causing very severe blast damage to Nos. 141 to 167 Coombe Road, Sussex Villa and Nos. 1 to 6 Coombe Avenue, Nos. 91 & 93 Park Hill Road and Nos. 2 & 3 Brownlow Road. Window and roof damage in varying degrees over a radius of 400 yds.
20/6/44	No 3 Chepstow Road	FLY	Small crater at rear of No. 18. This house and No. 20 partially wrecked. Nos. 14 & 16 Chepstow Road, No. 1 Chepstow Rise, and 18 Park Hill Rise were rendered unstable. Very severe blast damage was caused to No. 12 Chepstow Road & 2, 3, 5, & 7 Chepstow Rise. Blast damage was caused approximately 300 yds radius from the point of impact. Many large trees possibly minimised the full blast effect.
20/6/44	Coombe Road	FLY	Fell in carriageway, Heathfield Road 60 ft from Coombe Road. The following houses were wrecked: Nos. 1 & 3 Heathfield Road, 17 Coombe Road and part of Heathfield Flats facing Heathfield Road. "The Schola" and 5 Heathfield Road, 17 Coombe Road & No. 129 Edridge Road were partially wrecked. Nos. 7 & 9 Heathfield Road, part of Heathfield Flats and 92 Edridge Road were rendered unstable. Severe blast damage was caused to 84 to 90 and 111 to 127 Edridge Road, 2,4 & 20 Coombe Road and 2, 4, 11 & 13 Heathfield Road: also to Heathfield Gardens (flats) and No. 2 St. Peters Road. Blast damage was caused over a radius of 500 yds.
25/6/44	Addiscombe Road	FLY	Fell in garden at rear of No. 138. This house and 140 wrecked, No. 136 unstable, No. 134 partially unstable. Nos. 142, 144, 301 and 303 Addiscombe Road, No. 1 Mapledale Avenue and No. 2 Fryston Avenue seriously damaged. Blast damage was caused over a radius of 400 yds.
29/6/44	Lloyd Park Avenue	FLY	Detailed information cannot be found at present, however some photographs are available at the Local Studies library. Censorship prevented identifiable Newspaper reports.
1/7/44	Dalmally Road	FLY	Ditto
5/7/44	Estcourt Road	FLY	Ditto
7/7/44	Beckford Road	FLY	Ditto
7/7/44	Handley's Brickworks	FLY	Ditto
21/7/44	Estcourt Road	FLY	Ditto
27/7/44	Bredon Road	FLY	Ditto
7/8/44	Ranmore Avenue	FLY	Ditto
26/1/45	Lloyd Park	V2 Rocket	6.07 p.m. Coombe farm. In field. Blast damage to Army Camp, 2 injured. (Could this be the incident involving the AA guns at North of Mapledale Ave.?)

BOMB PATCHES AND ALL THAT
by Paul Nihill

The kids of today have their mobile phones, computers, videos and CD players, etc. to keep them amused, and yet they still complain of being bored. In my young days just after the Second World War we had to find our own fun with far lesser things; cigarette cards, marbles, a set of dabs and – if you were lucky – a pair of roller skates was about all you'd own in those days.

We did, however, have one activity that today's young-un's will never be able to enjoy. That was playing on bomb patches and for that pleasure we didn't have to pay one penny. Parks were fun but a bomb patch offered so much more. In and around Addiscombe were five such bomb patches, areas where several properties had been destroyed by those nasty Germans. There were two such sites in Lower Addiscombe Road very close to where we lived. **No. 1** at the top of Warren Road was the first bomb patch I ever played on. Warren Court now stands on the site. Prior to being bombed six shops embracing 73 to 83 Lower Addiscombe Road stood there. This wasn't a particularly large site – but it was a good one as it was here every Guy Fawkes Night that a huge bonfire was erected. We kids would for weeks gather up any thing that would burn and pile it up. I remember one year it was so big the Council or some-body made us pull half of it down. Once the fire had been lit all the locals would set off their fireworks providing a super display that would be hard to match anywhere. (See Bomb Table 19/4/41)

Down the other end of Lower Addiscombe Road directly alongside The Black Horse Public House was a similar sized bomb patch **No. 2** where once stood seven shops. On occasions when my mother gave me my bus fare home from school I would play on this patch whilst waiting for a 12 or 59A bus. Needless to say I got so involved with enjoying myself that I never noticed the dozen or so buses that would pull up and depart without me. To be honest I'd have got home a lot quicker had I walked. (See Bomb Table 27/9/40)

At **No. 3** in Chepstow Road there was a very large bomb patch that spread along to Chepstow Rise and up to Chichester Road. This was a truly fantastic adventure playground with plenty of places to hide. I spent many happy hours here. On this patch you could act out all your Wild West cowboy fantasies. (Probably Bomb Table 20/6/44)

A little further along Chepstow Road you turn left up Park Hill Road to **No. 4**. This was another fairly large site which gave us so much pleasure exploring. It is a pity all the bomb patches were eventually built on because they were such exciting places to visit. (Probably Bomb Table 29/9/40)

Nearby in Stanhope Road by Park Hill was a very large bomb patch **No. 5** that to us resembled a jungle. It was wild and overgrown. The patch extended to Fairfield Path which we always knew as one of the seven alleys that started at East Croydon and ended up at Lloyd Park. It was like a Hollywood Tarzan film lot. (Probably Bomb Table 28/9/40)

On 8 November 1940 a high-explosive bomb caused damage to property in Ashling Road and Lower Addiscombe Road resulting in a small bomb patch **No. 6** opposite Woolworths. This area to us was always known as Bingham Halt. My mum bought me some gold paper chains that I hid in a hole on the site. This must have been Christmas 1944 or 1945.

Two bomb sites I remember visiting on my journeys to and from school were at Capri Road **No. 7** which was bombed on 16 April 1941 causing a lot of destruction to houses in the vicinity. The other site **No. 8** was a small one in Blackhorse Lane where two houses were demolished on 8 March 1941. There were other exciting bomb sites that I played on but they were outside the Addiscombe area.

I have tried without success to pinpoint the month or year that I moved to Addiscombe. I have always believed it was late in 1943, or early 1944, but to be honest I don't know when it was. One night our windows in Lower Addiscombe Road were blown out and upon checking 'The Borough Engineer's Report on Air Raid Damage 1940–1944' the only incident I can think of that would have caused the damage occurred on 23 February 1944 when incendiary bombs were scattered over a wide area near Lower Addiscombe Road. To add to the mystery of when I was first in Addiscombe I clearly can remember picking up dead mice from bomb ruins. But the bombing of all the sites I have mentioned were bombed at least two years previously to when I believed I moved to Addiscombe (and the dead mice would have all disappeared by then). The patch **No. 3** in Chepstow was more recent, but I never sought out mice there. It doesn't add up – but I did used to look on the sites for dead mice, and that is a fact.

Today whenever I walk by the sites where the old bomb patches were, and where houses, shops or flats now stand I cannot help but think back to the days when there was just rubble and overgrown trees and weeds. Yeah, we sure had some fun on those bomb patches.

Subscribers

Mrs Evelyn M. Adams, Addiscombe, Surrey
Michael F. Allain, Addiscombe, Surrey
Valerie Allen, Nowra, New South Wales, Australia
Ray Anderson, Croydon, Surrey
Mrs Jennifer Andreas, East Croydon, Surrey
Marianna Ascott, St Mary's Choir member (until 1998)
Paul and Tina Austin, Addiscombe, Surrey
Mrs Ivy Ayling, Addiscombe, Surrey
Mr Doug Geden, Simone and Jack Bailey, Croydon, Surrey
Mrs Gladys Bailey, Croydon, Surrey
J. H. Bainbridge, Addiscombe, Surrey
Alan and Jean Barber, Shirley, Croydon, Surrey
Mr and Mrs Barker, Addiscombe, Surrey
Liam and Ellie Barlow, Croydon, Surrey
Lyn Barnett, Shirley, Surrey
The Barthaud family, Whitgift Estate, Croydon, Surrey
Jacqueline and Keith Bartley, Addiscombe, Surrey
David G. Bate, Keyworth, Nottingham
Heather and Christopher Bates, Addiscombe, Surrey
Don Bates
Pat and Alan Bates, Addiscombe, Surrey
Marion and George Battley, Addiscombe, Surrey
Mr and Mrs R. Beagley, Addiscombe, Surrey
Terence A. Bing, Shirley, Croydon, Surrey
C. A. Bircham, Addiscombe, Surrey
Richard Blackwell, Addiscombe, Surrey
John Beresford Blunsden, Whitgift Foundation, Addiscombe, Surrey
Pam Bone, Toggles, Warlingham Green
Mr L. A. Bradbury and Mrs W. J. Harper, Park Hill, Croydon, Surrey
Mrs Kathleen Brandon, Addiscombe, Surrey
Geoff and Joan Brashier, East Croydon, Surrey
Gary Brashier, Croydon, Surrey
Paul Brashier, Croydon, Surrey
Mrs G. C. Braund, Isle of Wight
K. and J. Brazier, Croydon, Surrey
Roger and Jacinta Bridge
Colin Broad, Addiscombe, Surrey
Mr John M. Broderick, Addiscombe, Surrey
Barbara Broughton, Addiscombe, Surrey
Malcolm Brown, Button House, Addiscombe, Surrey
John W. Brown, Local History Publications
Emma C. Budgen, Addiscombe, Surrey
Bertha Bull (née Henbest), Peacehaven
Terence Burgess, Addiscombe, Surrey
George Bush, Addiscombe, Surrey
Mr and Mrs M. C. Bushell, Shirley, Surrey
Dick and Sarah Butcher, Addiscombe, Croydon
Mrs F. S. Butcher, Oxted

P. C. Butt, Croydon, Surrey
Nigel Callow, Addiscombe, Croydon, Surrey
Mr and Mrs K. A. Campbell, Addiscombe, Surrey
Anthony John Cane, Addiscombe, Surrey
William Canning, Dunsilly Lodge, Antrim
Mr P. J. Card, Addiscombe, Surrey
Donald Carmichael, Addiscombe, Surrey
Michael J. Carpenter,
Molly and Gerd Carrington, Addiscome, Surrey
Mrs Margaret E. Carter-Pegg (née Mant), South Croydon, Surrey
Eric Chalkley, St James Lodge, Addiscombe, Surrey
Mrs Barbara Charters, Toronto, Canada
Dr Duncan Charters, Elsah, Illinois, USA
M. A. Christopher, Addiscombe, Surrey
Pamela Clark, Addiscombe, Surrey
Jill H. Clarke, Addiscombe, Surrey
Robin and Susan Clarke, Croydon, Surrey
Sylvia J. Clements
Graham and Adrienne Cluer, Addiscombe, Croydon, Surrey
Michaela Coelho, Addiscombe, Surrey
Robert Cogger, Addiscombe, Croydon, Surrey
Fiona Coiley, Addiscombe, Surrey
Stephen A. Cole, Addiscombe, Surrey
Edward Cole, Woodside
Clive Richard Coles, Capri Road, Addiscombe, Surrey
Arthur J. Colley, Addiscombe, Surrey
Maureen and Stephen Collins, Addiscombe, Croydon, Surrey
Ron Collyer, Addiscombe, Surrey
Mrs L. Cook, Addiscombe, Surrey
Mrs K. Cooper
Terry Cooper, Sheffield
William G. Cooper, Croydon, Surrey
William (Bob) Corner, Addiscombe, Surrey
M. Cowan, Addiscombe, Croydon, Surrey
Mrs J. Cowland, Addiscombe, Surrey
Maureen Critchley, Croydon, Surrey
Eileen F. Crowe, Ide Hill, Kent
Croydon Natural History and Scientific Society, Croydon, Surrey
Mrs Rosie D'Costa
Miss Muriel D'Rozario, Addiscombe, Surrey
Mrs W. E. M. Darch
Julie Davidson, Addiscombe, Surrey
A. J. Davies
R. R. Davis
Melanie De Villiers, Addiscombe, Croydon
Mrs Olive F. Dear, Addiscombe, Surrey
Mr and Mrs D. Dear

Ernest Denning, Addiscombe, Surrey

Alison Dennis, Great Dunmow, Essex

Laurie and Gigi Devereaux, Addiscombe, Croydon, Surrey

Jacqueline Y. Dickinson, East Croydon, Surrey

Ian Dixie, Addiscombe, Surrey

John Dixon, St Ouen, Jersey

John Dixon, Addiscombe, Surrey

Alan Dolton, Addiscombe, Surrey

Graham Donaldson, Croydon, Surrey

Andrew and Margaret Donovan, Addington, Surrey

James Drinkwater, Cecil Court, Croydon, Surrey

Valerie J. Dummons, Croydon, Surrey

Gary S. Edwards, Addiscombe, Surrey

Paul and Sandy Elliott, Addiscombe, Surrey

Peter G. Etheridge, Addiscombe, Surrey

Brenda Evans (née Roebuck), Croydon, Surrey

Anne P. Fahey, Croydon, Surrey

S. J. Farage, Croydon, Surrey

Mr and Mrs A. Fathipour,

Graham A. Feakins, Herne Hill, London

David J. Fearn, Addiscombe, Surrey

Lynne Feeney and Family, Addiscombe, Surrey

David G. Fenner, Addington, Croydon, Surrey

Asoka Fernando

Mr R. and Mrs K. Few, Fareham, Hants.

Mr and Mrs R. Field, Addiscombe, Surrey

Rev. Timothy Finigan, Blackfen

Joan M. Fitter, Addiscombe, Surrey

Councillor Jerry Fitzpatrick, Addiscombe, Surrey

Iris Flint, Coulsdon, Surrey

Jackie Forwood, Addiscombe, Surrey

Sharon L. Fox, Brixham, Devon

Mr Ian A. Francis, Addiscombe, Surrey

Revd D. J. and Mrs C. A. Frost, St George's Vicarage, Shirley

Roger Fuller, Chineham, Basingstoke

Andrew Fuller, Ilminster, Somerset

Alan Galer, Upfield, Croydon, Surrey

The Gallard Family, Grant Road, Addiscombe, Surrey

Chris Gee, Churchwarden, Addiscombe Parish Church

John B. Gent, Croydon, Surrey

Barbara M. George, Addiscombe, Surrey

Philip Gibson, Addiscombe, Surrey

Roger and Ruth Gledhill, East Croydon, Surrey

Mr R. C. Godden, Addiscombe, Surrey

Mr W. A. G. and Mrs J. F. Goddin, Hastings

Lois J. Godwin, Addiscombe, Surrey

Anthony Gomesz, Addiscombe Court Road

Elizabeth Goodall (née Coleman), formerly Addiscombe, Croydon, Surrey

Martin Gordon, Addiscombe, Surrey

Stan Goron, Addiscombe, Croydon

Diana Gorton, Addiscombe, Surrey

Mr J. Greasley, Croydon, Surrey

Peter R. Green, Shirley, Croydon, Surrey

Mark John Green, Addiscombe, Surrey

Christopher John Green, Addiscombe, Surrey

David A. W. Green, Addiscombe, Surrey

Tony Hacche, Meadvale Road, Croydon, Surrey

Dianne S. Haile

Mr Warren Hall, Croydon, Surrey

Charles Hamilton, Addiscombe, Croydon

Derry-Anne and Paul Hammond, Canning Road, Croydon, Surrey

R. A. Handscombe, Addiscombe, Surrey

John Hanson, Croydon, Surrey

Tim Harding, South Croydon, Surrey

Mr and Mrs Anthony E. Hardstone,

Ken Harman, Sanderstead, South Croydon, Surrey

David Harmes, Addiscombe, Surrey

Winifred Harrington, Addiscombe, Croydon, Surrey

Mr and Mrs C. M. Harris, South Norwood, SE25

Miss G. F. Harrison, Addiscombe, Surrey

Miss Naomi Harrison, Addiscombe, Surrey

Jeremy G. Harrison, Addiscombe, Surrey

David A. Harwood, Addiscombe, Surrey

Mr Peter Hassard, Addiscombe, Surrey

Henry G. Hawkins,

Hayes/Clare family, Addiscombe, Surrey

E. J. Hayward, Croydon, Surrey

Mr David Healy, Addiscombe, Surrey

Doreen and Christopher Hedgcombe, Addiscombe, Surrey

Mrs Muriel Hevey, Paul Gardens, Croydon, Surrey

Mrs J. D. Hibbert, Croydon, Surrey

Mrs O. Hibbert, South Norwood

A. B. Holding, Addiscombe, Surrey

Marc Holland

The Holt family, Capri Road, Addiscombe, Surrey

Neville Hortas, Addiscombe, Surrey

Andrew Howard, Addiscombe, Surrey

Melinda Hunneybun-Ashford,

Roger Hurrion, Addiscombe, Surrey

Mr Anil Idnani, Purley, Surrey

Tracey and Phil Insuli, Addiscombe, Surrey

Ian Isham, Park Hill, Croydon, Surrey

Mr F. Jackson

Nicola S. James, Croydon, Surrey

Doreen M. James, Addiscombe, Surrey

Katie Jeffs, Addiscombe, Croydon

N. Johnceline, Croydon, Surrey

K N. Johnceline, Wenhaston, Suffolk

Mr and Mrs R. Johnson, Shirley, Croydon, Surrey

Babs and John Jones, Addiscombe, Surrey

John A. Jones, Addiscombe, Surrey

Tom and Barbara Karelis, Addiscombe, Surrey

Lesley K. E. Kavanagh, Addiscombe, Surrey

Anne R. Keeley, Addiscombe, Croydon, Surrey

Reg Kemp, Morden, Surrey

Dennis and Marjorie King, Hailsham

Patrick, Mary and Clare Kingman, Addiscombe, Surrey

James Kingswell, Wallington, Surrey

Mr J. Kirkby

Robert M. Krarup, Addiscombe, Surrey

Patrick Charles Lane, Addiscombe, Surrey

Mr and Mrs P. C. Lane, Addiscombe, Croydon, Surrey

David P. Lane, Addiscombe, Croydon, Surrey

Paul Derrick Lane, Addiscombe, Surrey

David Patrick Lane, Addiscombe, Surrey

Mr L. C. Leeder

Mrs Mary Leney, Addiscombe, Surrey

Ashley Lenton, Addiscombe, Surrey

D. Leriche, Addiscombe, Surrey

Mrs D. M. Lewis, Croydon, Surrey

Margaret S. Lewis, Park Hill, Croydon

Nora G. Lewis (née Nash), Uttoxeter

A. Loft, Addiscombe, Surrey
London Surfacing Co. Ltd, Croydon, Surrey
R. J. Long, Addiscombe, Surrey
Sylvia Lover, Park Hill, Croydon
Glen Lucas and Lisa Hungerford,
Maria Lynn, Addiscombe, Surrey
Colin and Patricia Lyon, Addiscombe, Surrey
Pauline Macbroom, Croydon, Surrey
Fraser S. Macdonald, Shirley, Surrey
Sheila Macfarlane, formerly of Woodside Green
Miss S. Malyon, Croydon, Surrey
Martyn Mance, Addiscombe, Surrey
Mrs Molly Mant (née Glazier), South Croydon, Surrey
Roger G. Marshall, Shirley Park, Croydon, Surrey
Peter D. Maryan, Addiscombe, Surrey
Mr S. V. and Mrs Masters, Birchanger Road,
    South Norwood, London
James McArdell, Addiscombe, Surrey
Patrick W. McCarthy
Mr and Mrs J. McHale, Addiscombe, Surrey
Stephen P. McHugo, Addiscombe, Surrey
Graham Medcalf, Addiscombe, Surrey
Mr and Mrs B. Mills, Birchanger Road, South Norwood,
    London
Shirley Mills, Outram Road, Croydon, Surrey
James Milmoe, Addiscombe, Croydon
Barbara Mitchell, Camberley, Surrey
R. Morley, Addiscombe, Surrey
C. Morley-Smith, Addiscombe, Surrey
Miss Jolie Florence Morris, Ashburton Road,
    Addiscombe, Surrey
Tony Moss, Park Hill, Addiscombe, Surrey
Bryan A. Netherwood, East Croydon, Surrey
Mary Neville-Kaye O.B.E., Addiscombe, Surrey
Mr and Mrs T. W. Newman, Addiscombe, Surrey
Mrs R. Newnham
Nichola and David Nicholls, Addiscombe, Surrey
Ann and Ken Nicholson, Addiscombe, Surrey
Paul Nihill, formerly of Addiscombe, Surrey
Robert Oliver, ex Craigen Avenue, Addiscombe, Surrey
Tina T. Overton, Addiscombe, Surrey
Linda C. Owen, Canning Road, Addiscombe, Surrey
Mrs E. Pamphilon, Addiscombe, Surrey
Mr Alex Pang, Addiscombe, Surrey
Deborah Maria and Nicholas Bateson Parden,
    Addiscombe, Surrey
Sarah M. Parshall, Addiscombe, Surrey
A. Patterson, Addiscombe, Surrey
John Pauling, Wold Newton
Catherine Peck, Canning Road, Addiscombe, Surrey
Mr and Mrs B. J. L. Pentecost, Addiscombe, Surrey
Rachel Perrins, East Croydon, Surrey
Gillian and Michael Perrins, Addiscombe, Surrey
Mr and Mrs Sean N. E. Phillips, Addiscombe, Surrey
Michael Pickett, Croydon, Surrey
Jim Pickett, Addiscombe, Surrey
Mr Edward F. G. Potter, Shirley, Croydon, Surrey
Barry P. Press, Addiscombe, Surrey
Mr B. E. Price, Croydon, Surrey
A. J. Prosbik, Croydon, Surrey
Violet Ellen Ramsey, Addiscombe, Surrey
Mr and Mrs L. M. Ramsey, Addiscombe, Surrey
Mr Michael Reason, Shirley, Croydon, Surrey
Carl X. F. Rich, East Croydon, Surrey

Mary Riches, Addiscombe, Surrey
Elizabeth Ritchie, Addiscombe, Surrey
Suzanne Rixon, Addiscombe, Surrey
Elizabeth and David Robbins, Addiscombe, Surrey
Paul Roberts, Park Hill, Croydon, Surrey
Shirley Roberts, Old Coulsdon, Surrey
Sheila Roberts-Morgan, Addiscombe, Surrey
Steve and Carol Rodway, Addiscombe, Surrey
Brian Roote, Whyteleafe, Surrey
Mike Ross, Addiscombe, Surrey
B. Rudge, Addiscombe, Surrey
Joyce Russell (née Stredwick), Earley
'Nigel' Derek Warren Ryan, Addiscombe, Surrey
Mary Salter, Addiscombe, Surrey
Mrs M. C. Scherr
Miss J. M. S. Scherr
Michael Semeta, Addiscombe, Surrey
Maurice and Ivy Shakespeare, Capri Road, Addiscombe,
    Surrey
Helena and Michael Shiatis, Croydon, Surrey
Susan E. Shillabeer, Addiscombe, Surrey
Gary J. Shirley, Croydon, Surrey
Monica Shuttleworth
Tony Simpkin, Addiscombe, Surrey
B. and C. Simpson, Addiscombe, Surrey
John Skillicorn, Croydon, Surrey
Tony Skrzypczyk, Addiscombe, Croydon
Nuala and Robert Smith, Canning Road, East Croydon
Jodie Smith, New Addington, Surrey
Peter Jervis Smith, Croydon, Surrey
Mrs M. E. Smith, Park Hill, Croydon, Surrey
Susan J. Smith, Croydon, Surrey
Joyce Smith (née Wawman), Addiscombe, Surrey
Rose Snashfold, Addiscombe, Croydon, Surrey
Steve, Lynn Sophia, Dan and Joseph, Upfield, Croydon,
    Surrey
Paul W. Sowan, South Croydon, Surrey
P. Stanton, Addiscombe, Surrey
J. Stanton, Orpington, Kent
Mr A. Steele, formerly of Croydon, Surrey
Martin J. Sterling, Addiscombe, Surrey
Mr Robert J. Stokoe, Morland Road, Croydon, Surrey
Gladys Stoner, Addiscombe, Surrey
Rev. Gerry Stongal
Robert A. Streeter, Addiscombe, Surrey
John Stretton, Addiscombe, Surrey
Andrew E. Strevens, Addiscombe, Surrey
Beryl M. Suckling (née Pauling), Woodstock
Margaret Surrey, Addiscombe, Surrey
Mark J. Swain, Addiscombe, Surrey
Sid and Joyce Swain, Addiscombe, Surrey
Dawn Symes, Croydon, Surrey
Mr Paul F. Tappenden, Kingscote Road, Addiscombe,
    Surrey
Heather Tarling, Blackhorse Lane, Croydon, Surrey
Joseph F. Taylor, Shirley, Croydon, Surrey
D. Tedder, East Croydon, Surrey
Terraquest Group Plc
Mr Jason Thomas, Addiscombe, Croydon, Surrey
Jill Thomas (née Connolly), Oval Road, Croydon,
    Surrey
Gordon Thompson, Addiscombe, Surrey
The Thomson Family, Addiscombe, Surrey
Margaret E. Todman, Addiscombe, Surrey

SUBSCRIBERS

Anne Tompsett, Croydon, Surrey
Alan J. Tomsett OBE, Croydon, Surrey
Paul Tunnell, Addiscombe, Surrey
Sylvia B. Turner, Addiscombe, Surrey
Mrs S. L. and Mr D. H. Turner,
Rhoda K. Twin, Addiscombe, Surrey
Mrs Janet S. Twomey, Addiscombe, Surrey
Enid Willson Vigor
Rex E. Vimont, Addiscombe, Surrey
Eileen Vince (née Beach), Addiscombe, Surrey
Peter Walker, Croydon, Surrey
Eileen O. Walkin, Addiscombe, Surrey
John F. W. Walling, Newton Abbot, Devon
Mr Keith G. Walton, Addiscombe, Surrey
Mr Matthew Want, Addiscombe, Surrey
Ms J. Ward, Addiscombe, Surrey
Martin P. Ware, Addiscombe, Surrey
Mrs K. E. Warwick, Addiscombe, Surrey
Norman J. Waters, Shirley, Croydon, Surrey
Malcolm Waters, Croydon, Surrey
Jeanne E. Watts, Addiscombe, Surrey
Stuart Weedon
Michael P. Weller, Woodside, Croydon, Surrey
Shirley and Charlie West, Selsdon Vale

Dave West, Addiscombe, Surrey
Janice West (née Beach), Addiscombe, Surrey
Keith White, Addiscombe, Surrey
Andrew White, Addiscombe, Surrey
Peter A. Whybrow
Lisa Jackson and Graham Williams, Capri Road,
    Addiscombe, Surrey
Mrs Leonora M. Williams, Addiscombe, Surrey
The Williams Family, Addiscombe, Surrey
Pamela Winters, Addiscombe, Surrey
Mrs D. J. Wood, Addiscombe, Surrey
Mr W. Wood, Shirley, Croydon, Surrey
Mrs Maureen Wood and Mr William G. Wood,
    Addiscombe, Croydon, Surrey
Mr and Mrs R. Woodman
Eva Woods, Shirley, Surrey
Margaret Woolf (née Beach), Addiscombe, Surrey
Mr William E. Wootton, Addiscombe, Surrey
Sandra and Stephen Wright, Croydon, Surrey
Nikki M. Yates, Addiscombe, Surrey
Darran M. Yates, Addiscombe, Surrey
Norman and Jenny Young, Addiscombe, Surrey
Frederick A. Younge
Barbara E. Zammit, Addiscombe, Surrey

KEY TO PICTURE CREDITS

A.B.   Anne Bridge
A.Bo.   Alma Boxhall
A.H.   Archie Handford
A.R.   Ann Roy, Croydon Natural History and
    Scientific Society
B.B.   Barbara Broughton
B.C.   Bob Corner
B.W.   Bill Wood
C.A.   Reproduced by kind permission of the
    Croydon Advertiser group.
C.I.   Christies Images
C.L.S.L.   Croydon Local Studies Library
C.T.   *Croydon Times*
D.D.   David Delaney
D.C.   Dudley Carey
E.H.   Edward Handley
E. and T.T.   Enid and Ted Thomas
H.B.   Harris & Bailey
H.C.   HarperCollins
H.V.   Henry Vibart, from *Addiscombe, Its Heroes
    and Men of Note*
I.A.   Ian Allen Publishing
I.W.M.   Imperial War Museum
J.G.   John Gent
J.H.   John Hobbs
J.K.   John Kavanagh
J.P.   Mr J Pentecost
L.   Lens
N.C.   Nigel J. Clark
N.S.   Norwood Society

P.N.   Paul Nihill
P.O.   Paul O'Callaghan
P.T.   *Pictorial Times*
R.H.   Rosa Hurn
R.W.   Ruth Watts
S.C.   Steve Collins
S.E.   Steve Earl
S.F.S.   Surrey Flying Services
S.H.   Steven Hobbs
S.M.R.B.   St Mildred's Record Books
S.P.   Surrey Press
T.I.L.N.   *The Illustrated London News*
T.P./B.   Tom Purvis/Bridgeman
T.S.   Tony Stelling
T.W.   Tony Wild

*Phillips shoe repairers opposite the Black
Horse. Mr Phillips is on the left and Mr F.
Nicolls is on the right.* (E. & T.T.)

AVAILABLE TO BUY NOW IN THE SERIES

The Book of Bampton, A Pictorial History of a Devon Parish • Caroline Seward
The Book of Bickington, From Moor to Shore • Stuart Hands
The Parish Book of Cerne Abbas, Abbey and After • Vivian and Patricia Vale
The Book of Chittlehampton, A North Devon Parish • Various
The Book of Cornwood and Lutton, Photographs and Reminiscences • Compiled by the People of the Parish
The Ellacombe Book, A Portrait of a Torquay Parish • Sydney R. Langmead
The Book of Grampound with Creed • Amy Bane and Mary Oliver
The Book of Hayling Island and Langstone • Various
The Book of High Bickington, A Devon Ridgeway Parish • Avril Stone
The Book of Helston, Ancient Borough and Market Town • Jenkin with Carter
The Book of Ilsington, A Photographic History of the Parish • Dick Wills
Lanner, A Cornish Mining Parish • Scharon Schwartz and Roger Parker
The Book of Lamerton, A Photographic History • Ann Cole and Friends
The Book of Loddiswell, Heart of the South Hams • Various
The Book of Manaton, Portrait of a Dartmoor Parish • Compiled by the People of the Parish
The Book of Meavy, Dartmoor Parish, Village and River • Pauline Hemery
The Book of Minehead with Alcombe • Hilary Binding and Douglas Stevens
The Book of North Newton, In Celebration of a Somerset Parish • Robins & Robins
The Book of Plymtree, The Parish and its People • Tony Eames
The Book of Porlock, A Pictorial Celebration • D. Corner
Postbridge – The Heart of Dartmoor • Reg Bellamy
The Book of Priddy, A Photographic Portrait of Mendip's Highest Village • Various
The Book of Silverton, Portrait of An Exe Valley Parish • Silverton Local History Society
South Tawton and South Zeal with Sticklepath, 1000 Years Below the Beacon • Roy and Ursula Radford
The Book of Torbay, A Century of Celebration • Frank Pearce
Widecombe-in-the-Moor, A Pictorial History of a Dartmoor Parish • Stephen Woods
Uncle Tom Cobley and All, Widecombe-in-the-Moor • Stephen Woods
Woodbury, The Twentieth Century Revisited • Roger Stokes

SOME OF THE MANY TITLES AVAILABLE 2001

The Book of Bickleigh • Barrie Spencer
The Book of Blandford Forum • Various
The Book of Dawlish • Frank Pearce
The Book of Hemyock • Various
The Book of Hurn • Margaret Phipps
The Lustleigh Book • Tim Hall
The Book of Rattery • Various
The Book of Publow with Pensford • Various
The Book of Severn • Various
The Book of South Stoke • Various
The Book of Sparkwell • Pam James
The Book of Stourton Caundle • Philip Knott
The Book of Watchet • Compiled by David Banks
The Book of West Huntspill • Various

For details of any of the above titles or if you are interested in writing your own community history, please contact: Community Histories Editor, Halsgrove House, Lower Moor Way, Tiverton Business Park, Tiverton, Devon EX16 6SS, England Tel: 01884 243242/e-mail:sales@halsgrove.com